❖*To Be the Hands of God*

❖To Be the Hands of God

One Woman's Journey,
One Congregation's Challenge

Judy Griffith Ransom
with James G. Henderson

UPPER ROOM BOOKS
Nashville

To Be The Hands of God

Cover Design: Leigh Ann Dans
Cover Illustration: Tungwai Chau
First Printing: April 1992 (5)
ISBN 8358-0657-X
Library of Congress Catalog Card Number: 91-67170
Printed in the United States of America

❖

This book is dedicated to
Brian and Brent Henderson,
who gave their mother and me special strength
by showing us that miracles are everywhere—
you only have to look.

Jim Henderson

❖ Foreword

Judy Ransom has caught a ray of sunshine and used it to inspire and inform. She has written a story about a wonderful lady who knew how to live abundantly even as she walked through the valley of the shadow of death.

Joan Henderson had not lived in the shadows of life. She was a winner in life and her death was a victory of faith. We saw in Joan an example of God's love at work in a person. And that love was contagious, easily caught if you were around her. I think she taught us how to live and how to die.

Joan did not walk alone as she fought against almost impossible odds. Her husband and their sons were with her on the dangerous journey. Her friends joined her early, stayed until the end, and were blessed by the hours they had with her.

The story that is told here gives us a picture of the church at its best. From the first Sunday that Joan, Jim, Brian and Brent entered First United Methodist Church in Hendersonville, it was evident that they would be "doers of the word and not hearers only." The couple seated in front of them indicated that they too were first time visitors and at the end of the service Joan invited them to go home with her family for lunch. (I'm sure it was Joan who issued the invitation—no husband would dare!)

When the Friendship Sunday School Class, Joan and Jim's class, heard of Joan's sickness, they surrounded the family with love and care. The people in that class found a whole new meaning to their faith, not only in their reaction to the situation of the cancer, but in the way that they were able to help. It was an experience of community and of love that should always be in every church.

This book is more than the life of a remarkable young woman who inspired all who had the privilege of knowing her. It offers some very specific suggestions for all of us who will walk through the valley of the shadow of death with others before we make that trip ourselves.

Too often when a serious disease strikes, we gather our family, shut the door, and hide from the world. Our thoughts are turned on death rather than life as we wait for the inevitable. Joan and Jim gave their friends an opportunity to learn new lessons about living as they allowed them to help. In turn, the Hendersons experienced the love of God, not in the disease, but in the love of their friends and the wonderful healing work of the doctors, the nurses, and others who are a part of the healing institution.

This book offers us inspiration and information. I hope it will mean as much to you as it did to me.

Rev. Ben Alexander
Pastor of Visitation, First United Methodist Church
Hendersonville, Tennessee

❖ Author's Note

I can still see the card with the names of her family and telephone number that my neighbor pressed into my hand the morning I stood at the bus stop for the first time with my children, Audra and Whitney. She introduced herself as the school bus roared to a stop. Then she instructed her sixth grade son, "Brian, I want you to look out for these girls." As they stepped onto the bus that day I had no way of knowing that in a few years my children would be looking out for her—baking cookies, praying—and looking after themselves while I sat with her at the hospital.

Joan Henderson was the first person I met when we moved to Hendersonville, Tennessee, a city of 32,000 about twenty miles north of Nashville. We lived three houses apart in a middle class neighborhood, and during the next two years we got together occasionally with a handful of neighbors—also recent arrivals from various parts of the country—to hash over kids, school, career plans, and minor aches and pains.

Joan's cancer diagnosis shocked and scared me. Besides Brian, she and her husband Jim had another son, Brent, who was eight at the time of her diagnosis. I was scared for her and her family. They were so far from her parents, brother and sister, and so far from her longtime friends. Who would help her? What would happen to her family?

From the first day Joan and I met our relationship was characterized by light-hearted ribbing that grew to include a deep undercurrent of care. There seemed to be an "I'm there for you" understanding that went beyond taking the kids to school when they missed the bus or a shared ride to a luncheon, but it had never been tested. As Joan's cancer treatment began I knew that I would intentionally care for her. I also knew that I would have to look for ways to help since this spirited, self-sufficient friend would not be making lists of things to help with.

Who would care? What would happen to her family? I had never known anyone with a serious, long-term illness and yet I felt an answer within myself and saw an answer taking shape before my eyes—within the Sunday school class we both were a part of, within our church, within our neighborhood, and within our community. God's gift of caring was grown from good intentions to concrete actions.

As a newspaper feature writer, I kept thinking what a beautiful story was unfolding—not the story of Joan's cancer itself, but her reaction to it and the reactions of those around her.

Joan and I spent many, many hours together as her life changed and she remained home more and more. I had countless questions about dealing with cancer as a mother of young children—and we taped our conversations for later use. "Those are very good questions," Joan said one afternoon when we finished.

"Thank you," I replied, waiting.

"Did you get them out of a book?" she asked, that sly smile pulling at the corners of her mouth.

When she talked about giving a stewardship talk to a nursing friend's Sunday school class, I suggested she have it videotaped. She was a deep thinker, and I knew whatever she had to say could help others. A psychologist friend in our Sunday school class felt the same way, and taped an interview with her about life with cancer for future use. Joan spoke to our church and a videotape was made that is now in use by our local hospice.

Her college newspaper heard what was happening to her and Joan agreed to do an interview. She had filled up dozens of handwritten pages about her feelings during her cancer fight and asked me to type them for her. As I read her words, "I want so much to have mattered in this business of living," it came to me that Joan's story needed to be told. I went to Charlie Flood, a publisher friend who knew Joan, showed him Joan's notes and asked what he thought. "It needs to be a book," he said. Soon after, Charlie, Joan's husband Jim, and I sat down with Charla Honea and Lynne Deming of Upper Room Books.

Joan did not live to see her story written or published. But she knew we would try—and so she openly and eagerly shared her thoughts. She had always planned to get well enough to tell her story to help others.

Jim spent many hours reliving their life with cancer, sharing his feelings, so that others could know what is happening with and to the spouse. Others too shared soon after her death—for what they had seen happen with Joan, the outpouring of love in action, was something they wanted to see happen over and over.

❖

I owe a special debt of gratitude to all who helped us make Joan's book a reality: Cheryl Dismukes, Dr. Fernando Miranda, Dr. Gerald Davis, Mary MacArthur, Claudia Douglass, Patsy Lawson, Diana Diaz, the Rev. Ben Alexander, members of The Friendship Class and members of First United Methodist Church, and Joan's family, neighbors and friends. And I offer a sincere thank you to my editor, Robert Benson, and a host of family and friends who believed in and encouraged me.

Judy Griffith Ransom
1 March 1992

❖ One

She took a deep breath and smiled. Sunlight pouring through the dozen two-story windows that lined the cream colored walls added a warm glow that chill November morning. "Every movie has a rating, right? You check them before you send your kids. Well, this talk has a rating scale too. Not PG or R or X. This morning's rating is PC—Possible Crying." Joan Henderson, her hands trembling and heart pounding, looked out over a packed First United Methodist Church and began to prepare her audience of 500 persons for her talk about life with cancer.

Short, dark hair framed Joan's pale face, her skin smooth and unlined. It was her eyes that caught and held her audience. Medium blue with dark specks accented by slightly arched, soft brown eyebrows, her eyes signaled honesty and warmth and accessibility. Her ready laugh, quick wit, and inclusive personality had drawn these people to her, but her ability to find the positive in life's most painful journey had captured their hearts.

Who was this Joan to whom the ministers had turned over an entire Sunday morning worship service and who caused every seat in the church to be filled? She was a young girl running up the lane to share a school day with her mom. She was a little sister trapped beneath her fallen pony as her big brother ran for help. She was a college student getting soaked in the rain with her future husband. She was a mom able to back a boat and trailer into the lake. She was a neighbor welcoming newcomers with freshly baked cookies and her phone number. She was a Sunday school class member cooking soup on a cold day at an outdoor work project to feed fellow class members.

She was also a forty-three-year-old child of God dying of cancer who had claimed God's promises and was sharing her testimony with her congregation.

"What I have found over the past twenty-two months is that tears are warm and round and soft, and anything with adjectives like that can't be all bad." The ease with which she spoke and the warm smile that punctuated her sentences underscored the truth in Joan's words.

Throughout the audience were members of her Sunday school class, the bell choir, the men's club, neighbors and friends, many who had shared in the organization of a support group for Joan and her family. Others were there to hear her remarkable story and now they were being made to feel comfortable by the friendly banter of this former Iowa farm girl turned professor and coach who was as much at home on a tractor as she was standing before a classroom full of college students.

"I am so glad you all are here," she continued in a strong voice, as all eyes followed her down the red carpeted center aisle of the church. "From the very first moment that I found out I had cancer, this church has surrounded us with love, prayers, and support. Whether you like it or not, I draw tremendous strength from you all the time, so selfishly I am glad you are here today because I can sap you for every ounce of energy that you've got, and, believe me, I need that."

Joan wore low-heeled shoes, a simple, soft blue jumper, and long sleeved blouse. Her only jewelry was her wedding band and small silver earrings. There was about her an aura of elegance mixed with exuberance as she turned and walked slowly up the five steps to a large blue leather wing chair placed in the center of the platform at the front of the sanctuary. Jim, her husband of twenty-one years, was seated on her right side. Their young sons and biggest supporters, Brian and Brent, sat on the front pew.

Weak from chemotherapy treatment that might buy her a few more months of life, her abdomen painfully distended by a buildup of cancerous fluid, Joan stood briefly before the congregation. Her doctor had not wanted to release her from the hospital that morning and certainly did not want her in a crowded church, but she had prevailed. Her audience did not know it, but the doctor had told Joan adamantly the day before, "I don't want you to be there with all those people and all those germs!"

Joan knew the opportunity would not come again for her to witness to her congregation. "Is this my decision?" she had asked him, then added emphatically, "It's so important to me. I've got to do this!"

"Of course it's your decision," her doctor had replied. They struck a deal. He would transfuse her with two pints of blood, and she would promise not to stand in a receiving line after she spoke. Still, she was risking a life-threatening infection.

An expectant hush fell over the church as Joan sat down. She spoke an undeniable truth, "Any one of you could be up here this morning, standing here, doing what I am doing, but for whatever reason, it's my time." This was her time to tell the church how she and Jim and Brian and Brent had found the strength to survive almost two years of intensive cancer treatments. It was her time to urge the congregation to begin to talk about death as a normal, everyday process. It was her time to thank her church for upholding their church vows and supporting her family during her long illness.

"God planned life as much as He planned death, and because of that I can go forward," she continued. Then through the next hour, listeners relived with Joan the events that began one cold January afternoon almost two years earlier when she learned she had cancer and had asked an associate minister from the church to tell the congregation to pray for her. That day had overflowed with emotion as she and Jim and their children cried hard, frightened, angry, questioning tears.

What the Henderson family did not know that day as they began their struggle to discover what cancer would mean in their lives was that a group of people—church members, casual friends, and neighbors—cried too when they heard Joan had cancer. Their thoughts had turned to the Henderson family daily, and they wept for the pain the family would surely endure. But along with the tears came the seed of a commitment to develop an organization to help this family in their tragedy as much as they would allow.

"One of the great things about this whole experience is that no matter what has happened, you have always, always, always been there for us," Joan continued. Supporters who barely knew her at the onset of her illness were thankful they had listened to the voice of God within them urging them to discover and to share their gifts with Joan. The listening and the sharing had made a difference in their lives. Memories of happy, sad, fearful, courageous, caring days intermingled in a congregation, that through Joan and her family, had learned the strength and wisdom and joy that come from sharing God's love in practical ways.

What the congregation saw in Joan's eyes that morning was triumph, not defeat. The truth in her message was expressed perfectly in the words of the choir's opening anthem, "I Have Felt the Touch of God." The first stanzas mirrored Joan's feelings for her church and community:

> I have felt the touch of God through your hands.
> I've seen His look of love through your face.
> I have stood before his throne in your prayers.
> Because you cared, I've found God's grace.
>
> When I saw no hope in daily living,
> you reached a hand of tenderness and care.
> Darkness turned to light, a new day dawning.
> The joy of finding peace is why I share.

The last stanza reflected the congregation's feeling toward Joan.

> I have learned to trust the Lord through your faith.
> Your faithful walk with Him I clearly see.
> I have heard Him speak to me through your voice.
> Your love for Christ has helped to set me free.

Church members enriched by the Hendersons' acceptance of their prayers, love, and physical support were comforted with the assurance that at First United Methodist that same caring ministry could be available to them. And Joan, now serenely walking with her family toward the communion rail, began the end of her journey and faced death with the dignity that comes from love and acceptance of self and others.

❖

How different life had been two years earlier when Joan was in the audience of a huge hotel meeting room at the Pella Window National Convention in Scottsdale, Arizona. That day, it was Jim speaking in front of a large gathering. Dressed in a dark blue business suit, starched white shirt, and dark tie, he looked trim and healthy and happy. And why not? He and Joan had started a growing window installation business to complement the Pella Window distributorship Jim managed. While Jim managed the installation business, Joan worked up some of the quotes and handled the books, a perfect setup for parents of young, active children. The venture had proved so successful that Jim had been invited to give a presentation that morning. He sounded knowledgeable and confident as he explained to the crowd of businessmen how the two businesses could be successfully combined.

The trip to the Arizona convention marked a high point in Jim's life. He and Joan had a beautiful marriage and two great kids. Business was good, and they had finally been able to give a sizable gift to their church—all the windows in the new Family Life Center. In many ways, it seemed life for the Hendersons was the best it had ever been. Joan's parents had made a special trip to Tennessee to take care of the boys for the week so that she and Jim could attend the convention and celebrate their success together.

As Jim finished his speech he looked at Joan in the audience and he returned her smile. A round of hearty applause told him his message had been well received. "That was great; good delivery," she said, giving his hand a brief squeeze as he took his seat next to her.

Her respect was important to him. Throughout their twenty-one years of marriage, and even before, they had both been extremely competent. They valued each other's career and what their spouse was able to accomplish outside their marriage relationship.

As the audience awaited the next speaker, Jim's mind wandered back over the years that he and Joan had been together. They had met at Central College in Pella, Iowa. Jim, a quarterback for his Joliet, Illinois, high school football team, wanted to attend a small liberal arts college where he could continue to play football. He was offered a scholarship at Central by a head coach whose organizational skills and drive to succeed had a lifelong influence on him.

Joan was an above-average student and had grown up as one of three children on a one-hundred-year-old "Century Farm" in Montezuma, Iowa. She had earned money through the years as a 4-H member, raising and showing calves to sell at the local county fair. With the money she had earned, she had partially paid for her schooling. Friends and neighbors were delighted when Joan was named homecoming queen at Central. Homecoming day was a perfect day for football, cool and sunny, but on the farm it was seed corn picking time. Neighbors, in small town fashion, came and picked corn at Joan's parents' farm so her family could enjoy the day with her.

A sudden tragedy, the death of a member of the college football team the week before homecoming, had shocked the small campus. Students walked around dazed. As homecoming queen, Joan had prepared a happy, upbeat kind of speech for the coronation ceremony that would be held the Friday evening before the football game. Quickly, she rewrote her speech. When she addressed the student body at her coronation, she emphasized the family atmosphere of Central College, reminding both students and faculty that, like a family, they needed to come together and to support one another through a sad and difficult time.

Although Jim knew Joan through school activities and classes, an opportunity to work in Upward Bound, a summer program for underprivileged high school students, cemented their relationship. Both Jim and Joan had been assigned to the recreation department and they taught each of their assigned classes together. Together every day, sharing meals, chaperoning evening activities, strolling across the wooded 130-acre campus, they became best friends.

Later, Joan joined the faculty as a professor and gymnastics coach. Her solid listening and counseling skills attracted students to her, particularly the school's athletes who came to talk over problems and important decisions with her. She had her own ideas on education and the ability to make things simple. "We spend so much time teaching philosophy and theory of education that we never teach physical education majors how to get kids into a circle," she laughingly told Jim.

After graduation from Central, Jim continued his education at the University of Northern Colorado where he earned a master's degree in physical education and administration. He returned to Iowa as a high school football coach and then finally to Central College as an assistant coach. He found himself going to Joan, now his wife, for advice on how best to explain drills to his players. She had a knack for putting his concepts into words, and the back-and-forth exchange added to their marriage partnership.

With Joan working too, both contributed to the work of running the home. After their children were born they continued to do household chores together so that their free time could be enjoyed as a family.

The value of her family and the depth of her faith are evident in the letter Joan wrote the day that Brian was born:

> To me there is nothing quite so sweet as holding in my arms our newborn baby boy—to know he is our child, ours to love and care for, ours to clothe and feed, ours to teach and guide. But with the pride and joy also comes the realization that this child is going to face a world that is not very beautiful; and a baby is not a new toy but an immortal soul.
>
> I don't think I would have the courage to look our little baby in the face in light of today's headlines if it were not for the fact of an empty tomb, a risen Lord, and a philosophy of life that brings life into focus, gives beauty for ashes, and puts hope in the heart. When the days are uncertain, the future is sure. Because of a man called Jesus, I can look our little Brian in the face and say, "Because He lives, I can face tomorrow. Because He lives, all fear is gone." Because I know He holds Brian's future and ours, "life is worth the living, just because He lives."

Six years later, Brent was born in Pella, Iowa, and soon after they left their work at the college and moved to Knoxville, Tennessee, where Jim took a position with Pella Windows. The move was an upset for such a close-knit family. Joan had always been within two hours driving distance of her parents. "It's difficult to leave and exciting to go," they said as they prepared for the move.

The three years in Knoxville were tough ones. The young family never quite settled in and found their niche, and they wondered if they had made a mistake. Joan was no longer involved in a career, they had struggled to find a church group they were comfortable in, and they had to work hard to maintain a connection with home, sixteen hours away in Iowa. The one bright spot was the 1982 World's Fair that brought many friends from Iowa to visit.

A business opportunity in Nashville, Tennessee, made it necessary to relocate, and they settled into a brick, ranch style home in Hendersonville, twenty miles northeast of Nashville. The four-bedroom home was just right for the family. It was situated on a large, level lot and had a backyard that was perfect for football and baseball games. Gently sloping streets in the quiet, single-family neighborhood made bike riding and skateboarding a pleasure.

The move and a finished lower level in their new home brought an opportunity to help Joan's younger sister in a career move. Debra, who was married to a farmer in Iowa, wanted to pursue a career in mortuary science in order to supplement their income. It was an answer to prayer for Debra that Joan and Jim lived a half hour from her school and offered her a place to live.

Nine years younger than Joan, Debra had watched her sister become involved in cheerleading, music, drama, clubs, and other organizations that filled Joan's high school days. Debra had been proud to have Joan direct her junior choir where she learned a special lesson in giving. At the conclusion of practice for the Christmas program, Joan gave everyone a gift, a three-inch tall choir boy wearing a red choir robe with his mouth shaped in an "O." Most of the children unwrapped their candles and gave them no further thought but one little boy came up to Joan and bashfully thanked her for the gift. "It doesn't matter that the other kids didn't show appreciation," Joan told her sister later. "I'm just pleased to have given a gift that made a difference to one person."

When Joan and Jim lived in Pella, Debra spent many weekends with her sister baking cookies, shopping, talking, laughing. Joan was always the one to organize the family get-togethers—Mother's Days, birthdays, and Sunday dinners. "Meet us at the lake," was a favorite invitation of Joan's.

Debra's chance to again spend time with Joan and Jim and their children brought a new dimension to all their lives. Debra and Lindsey's son, Mitchell, was born while she attended school. Joan agreed to care for him the remaining eleven months before graduation, and the Hendersons developed a special bond with this new baby. Now all that was finished. Debra was back home in Iowa with her husband, and Joan was considering a return to school to pursue a master's degree in counseling.

Jim snapped back to the present as polite applause welcomed the next speaker. A half-hour later the morning presentations were over, and he and Joan made their way toward the banquet room accepting the congratulations of fellow distributors. Jim was on top of his world. Spring was coming, baseball season would soon start, and it would soon be time to open up the family's houseboat on Dale Hollow Lake.

As he and Joan squeezed through the doorway, someone jostled Joan, and she winced. As they had prepared for bed the previous night she had told Jim that the tiny thickening in her breast had suddenly become extremely tender. Already she had been to see the family doctor and had undergone a mammogram and a needle biopsy. Just to be sure, she had scheduled a regular biopsy for the day after they were to return home to have it checked again. Both the doctor and the technician had reassured them that from everything they were seeing, the thickening was not cancerous.

On Friday, January 29, 1988, Joan wrote: "One day surgery. Really nice people. Biopsy shows no cancer. Tissue looks healthy. The doctor felt really good about it. Dye test will be run over the weekend. Brian went on the church ski trip. I got sick from the anesthetic so I didn't get home as soon as they thought. Tired and sore, but okay."

The next day, Joan and Jim received preliminary reports that all the medical tests had come back negative for cancer, but the permanent section results were not yet available. Joan's parents felt a sense of relief at the good news and returned to Iowa.

❖

Joan's surgery for her biopsy put the Sunshine Committee of her Friendship Sunday School Class into action. Saturday morning, as Joan gingerly lowered herself into the leather recliner in her den, a classmate began a grocery list for the meal she had agreed to prepare for the Hendersons. As she left for the store, she said a prayer for Joan's quick recovery. Just as eight-year-old Brent found comfort in running for an extra blanket to tuck in around his mother, the classmate, nearer to Joan's age and with children Brian and Brent's ages, found comfort in helping Joan as well.

Joan spent most of Saturday resting as Brent watched cartoons and kept her company. She was young and healthy and would snap back in a day or two. Jim was there to help over the weekend, and Brian, at fourteen, was old enough to take care of himself. And yet members of the class, recognizing the need to enter into one another's problems, provided a meal—a simple, practical expression of love and concern. For those preparing the meal, the act of shopping, preparing, and delivering food was a reminder that someone was in trouble. Asking that the Henderson family would feel God's love and strength and that God would guide them in the best way to help was a natural prayer that day. Members delivering the food that night stayed only a few minutes, just long enough for Jim to share with the visitors that all the medical tests looked good. Sunday morning the class learned Joan was on the mend and feeling better.

The procedure that the Sunshine Committee had devised earlier worked efficiently. When the class had formed several years earlier, members voted to provide certain services and gifts for given situations. An overnight stay at the hospital rated flowers, balloons, a fruit basket, or a plant (with the cost not to exceed $20) and a visit by a committee member or class representative if possible. A class member who was ill at home received a card and phone call from a committee member inquiring about the situation and asking if help was needed with transportation, meals, or children.

Class members were as diverse as one might expect in a town most noted for its proximity to Music City U.S.A. The Friendship Class did have a Grand Ole Opry musician, but it also attracted teachers, writers, engineers, nurses, technicians, landscapers, salesmen, exercise instructors, office workers, and housewives, all with a common need to become known and to share a relationship with one another and with God. The class was committed to caring. A page in the class scrapbook spells it out:

> As long as we have memories,
> yesterday remains . . .
> As long as we have hope,
> tomorrow waits . . .
> As long as we have friendships,
> today is beautiful.

When it formed, the Friendship Class devised a format that allowed for a personal sharing time to enhance feelings of familiarity and connectedness. To this day, as the class session opens, members state their names and one good thing that happened during the week. Quickly names and faces merge, even for newer members, and individuals identify with one another as they share highlights in their lives. As the group became more accepting of one another, members began to open themselves up to new relationships.

A couple of challenging work projects, including the renovation of a home for victims of domestic violence, helped to make members three-dimensional instead of people in suits or dresses who offered polite good mornings and then sat stiffly sipping coffee on the back row of a Sunday school class. In addition to the major projects, members reached out through visiting nursing homes, providing Christmas baskets for needy families, collecting hats and mittens for the homeless, and securing cash donations in special needs cases.

One of the members tells this story about his attraction to the class. Joe and his wife Sandy were in the middle of a business transfer, and he had visited the class while she remained in Delaware. The morning was taken up with plans for a new project and business from an old project. Someone apologized afterwards for the absence of a lesson, but Joe was drawn to the group anyway. He had called Sandy that night and told her, "Here's a group doing something, putting their faith into action!"

The group's actions were certainly effective in helping those outside the class, but there was coming a time when the group would have to ask if it was meeting needs closer to home. One of the very vehicles instituted to promote caring in the group unwittingly blocked the free sharing of information and requests for help. Sharing one good thing that happened each week sent a message that bad things were not topics for discussion or sharing. And while zeroing in on acts of caring that required physical action, they were sometimes overlooking other ways that God gives people to care.

There are many gifts God gives his followers, says Duane Ewers, the author of *A Ministry of Caring*. "The Body of Christ is able to fulfill a ministry of caring because God has given the necessary gifts to members of the Body. God is the source of skills, abilities, and talents that are necessary for caring. Members of the Body of Christ are called to discover, affirm, and develop those gifts for a caring ministry. Some people seem to have natural gifts for caring. Others develop their gifts through affirmation, training and experience."

Ewers notes that God's gifts for caring include, "the ability to listen, to nurture, to accept, to be honest, to be available, to be patient, to keep confidences, to learn from one's own experiences of hurt, to identify with another and to be able to speak a word of hope in the midst of hurt and loss."

Although the need for knowledge of these special gifts of caring took a quantum leap as the next few months unfolded, no special training was instituted. Instead, the class reacted with its heart and provided for needs as they were discovered.

❖

We are a nation on the move with little in savings, little nearby family support, and health insurance that either does not cover policyholders completely or is non-existent. Split families, step-families, extended families, and no family at all—each add their own peculiar mix of problems and solutions. No wonder illness is scary. Roles are no longer rigidly defined and it is anyone's guess where support will be found in a crisis.

Regardless of the amount of money a person has when illness strikes, each still has the same twenty-four hours a day to get through. When considering types of services to provide an ill person or their family, we need to think about actions and services that will allow them time to spend time with the patient and their children, sleep, work, and participate in an enjoyable activity.

According to Abraham Maslow's hierarchy of human needs, people attain a sense of security through belonging, through association, through being accepted, through giving and receiving close friendship. First United Methodist members, as they began a new kind of interaction with the Henderson family, started to experience real agape love, the kind of love that stems from Christ within and does not depend upon the recipient.

The ham dinner delivered to the Hendersons' on early Saturday evening was delicious. It was the other half of a dinner enjoyed right up the street—easy to prepare and share. And yet, more than the physical food, it provided food for thought. For Joan and Jim and Brian and Brent, it meant that someone was thinking of them and was willing to meet their needs.

By evening Joan was feeling good. The day of rest had revived her and, as she curled up on the couch watching Jim wrestling with the boys on the den floor, she was reminded of how good her life was.

❖ Two

"Feeling better?" Jim asked, quickly closing the sliding door to the kitchen. He had slipped out of the house an hour earlier while everyone was still sleeping. He needed to run, his usual morning exercise, to release some of the tension brought on by Joan's surgery and too much inactivity that weekend. Their home was just a half mile from Old Hickory Lake. He loved to run along the road and watch the mist rise off the water as the sun came up.

"Good, really good, just a little sore," Joan said, handing him a glass of orange juice. She had gotten up, showered, then struggled into a soft pink jogging suit, white socks, and tennis shoes.

To Jim she looked fresh and energetic, ready for the day. "It's just been three days since the surgery, shouldn't you be taking it easy?" He worried about her doing too much too soon, but at the same time was proud of her for charging ahead.

"I'm fine," she reassured him, pulling packages and jars from the refrigerator as she prepared to make sandwiches for the boys' school lunches. "I'm expecting a call from the doctor today to set a time to get these stitches out." She glanced at her calendar. "Don't forget, this afternoon Brent has basketball practice at the church. I'll get him there if you'll come by and pick him up."

"It's a deal," Jim agreed. "Now, how about letting me make those sandwiches while you rest."

"I'm okay. Really. Just a little sore. Besides, you'd better get a move on or you'll be stuck in traffic."

An hour later Brian and Brent, school books in hand, collected the lunches and headed for the front door. From there they could watch for the school bus as it topped the hill coming toward the house, and thus avoid freezing at the bus stop across the road. "By the way, Mom, are you sure you're going to be okay with us in school?" Brian asked, poking his head back in the kitchen. A handsome, athletic young man, almost as tall as his parents, he had inherited his mother's even temper and ability to keep life in perspective without huge peaks and valleys.

"We could stay home and keep an eye on you," offered Brent, dark-haired like his big brother, and a bit more mischievous to boot. "It'd be hard not to go to school, but we could manage." An intense, excellent student, his moods swung from high to low like his father's.

Both boys would have liked nothing better than to stay home and spend the morning with their mom in the roomy kitchen. With its comfortable table, padded chairs, carpeted floor, wide counters, and sliding glass doors onto a second floor deck, the kitchen was a favorite gathering place.

"No such luck, you guys," Joan said, shaking her head as she walked them back to the front door. "Better run, here comes the bus now."

Her heart filled with joy as she watched her kids race across the yard. She had found each new stage the boys entered challenging but fun. Being a parent suited her. How lucky we are, she thought, watching her sons board the school bus. Soon this stupid lump business will be behind us. We have a healthy family, a successful business, the house payments are reasonable, and part of the boys' college is funded. She could not help thinking how good their life was. The ringing of the telephone broke into her thoughts, and she closed the door and hurried back to the kitchen.

"Hello," Joan answered as she sat down at the built-in desk that was squeezed between the refrigerator and the folding doors that hid a washer and dryer. Absentmindedly, she taped a photograph of her little nephew Mitchell to the side of the refrigerator, adding it to dozens of other family photos that made it look more like a family album than a storage place for food. "Yes, Doctor, I'll be in at 3:30 today," she told her surgeon. He had called to schedule a routine check of her stitches. Always a positive thinker, it did not occur to Joan that something might be wrong. She penciled in the appointment on her calendar next to Brent's scheduled basketball practice notation.

That afternoon, Joan sat overwhelmed and misty-eyed in an examining room at Dr. Davis's office as he told her one final test, the permanent section, had revealed traces of cancer in one lymph gland. She later wrote, "I felt as if I had been kicked in the face. My doctor was teary-eyed too as he outlined my best treatment option, a modified radical mastectomy to be performed immediately."

While some patients would have an option on the type of breast surgery performed, Joan did not. The large area of thickening and the detection of cancer in the thickening made the mastectomy her only choice.

Although shocked at Dr. Davis's words, her heart went out to him, he looked so sad. Without hesitating, she reached out to him as a friend and touched his arm as he rose to leave. "It must be very hard to say those words to someone," she said softly.

Numb from the surgeon's words, Joan slowly walked to her car and drove the three miles home to pick up Brent. One minute life was carefree and the future stretched ahead endlessly, the next—cancer! It was too late to call Jim at the office, she would have to wait until he brought Brent home from basketball practice to tell him. As she turned into her street, she spied Brent waiting for her on the front porch. He was dressed in shorts and a tee shirt covered by a school letter jacket. As she pulled into their driveway, he leaped the five steps to the walkway in typical eight-year-old exuberance. His irrepressible smile and good humor made her smile. He was a joy to be around. She tried to listen as he described his school day, but thoughts of cancer kept crowding in. She would tell Brent and Brian tonight, now was not the time.

"Why are you parking?" Brent asked as his mother stopped in front of the large, brick church a few minutes later.

"I want to talk to Ben," she said, giving him an affectionate pat. "Have a good practice, and your dad will bring you home after." She watched as he jogged over to the newly-built Family Life Center, flung open the door, and disappeared. Then she turned and walked toward the old church building that housed Brother Ben's office. A kindly, white-haired man nearing retirement, he had been the senior minister at the church when she and Jim joined four years ago. Not long after they had been saddened to learn that Ben's wife, Jerry, had terminal breast cancer. Both Jerry and Ben accepted the gifts of caring that the congregation poured out to them, reinforcing the members' efforts with gratitude. Even after Jerry's death, Ben constantly told the people of the church how right they were in their actions of caring.

Ben's attitude about cancer, his openness with the church, and the obvious comfort his faith gave him when tested were things that she and Jim had talked about. They had noticed the way that those things seemed to encourage people to connect with Jerry and Ben in both word and deed. Jerry's death had not left the congregation defeated. Instead, with Ben's feedback the congregation had become strong and confident in its ability to make a difference.

Ben would tell of a mystery person who delivered baskets of fruit during Jerry's illness and for months after her death. On Sunday he would say, "I don't know who you are, but thanks." The fruit gave him something to look forward to, but it was also a physical reminder that he was not alone, that someone was thinking of him.

And so it was to Ben that Joan went for support when she learned of the cancer, but his office door was locked. Her thoughts were interrupted by the associate pastor and a friend passing by in the hallway. "Joan, are you supposed to be out so soon after surgery?" they asked.

"I've just come from the surgeon's office—it's cancer."

Their faces registered shock as they reached to console her. In a few moments, the associate pastor spoke. "There's a church social tonight, and everyone will be asking how you're doing. Is there something we can tell people?"

"Tell them anything you want, I need all the prayers I can get."

❖

With that statement Joan opened a door through which so much love and support flowed that eighteen months later she wrote:

> If we open ourselves to the love and sensitivity of those who want to help us, we get such strength. You could probably even call what they do miracles. Our church in Hendersonville and our friends have truly been the hands of God. When we've been down

they have picked us up and carried us. I can hardly comprehend it, let alone explain it. They surround us with the unconditional love that gets us through. They anticipate and meet our needs each day.

I'm the lucky one. How many people in their lifetime are told by so many how much they are loved. These people are walking every step with us. I would feel so alone without them. I have never had the opportunity to feel alone because so many people have said, "We're here, we'll help you."

They are Christians in action, not just in words or empty vows that they make. What a priceless gift to give to somebody.

It would take some time for the Henderson family and First United Methodist to move toward an interdependent relationship and the joy it brings. Right now, time was something Joan intended to put to good use. The associate pastor promised to contact Brother Ben as Joan turned to leave.

Cancer. Surgery. Suddenly life was complicated. As she pulled out of the church parking lot, Joan began making mental lists of tasks she needed to accomplish: call her parents and ask them to come back; call her brother and sister; call their friends Sue and Jim in Iowa; do the laundry; let Judy know she would miss hand bell practice; pay the bills; go to the grocery store. Her organized, predictable life was suddenly chaotic. She needed to get home and start making plans, but first she must tell Jim and the boys.

Joan parked the station wagon behind the house and then leaned her head against the steering wheel, a momentary pause to calm herself. Brian was inside, and Jim and Brent would soon be on their way. Cancer, she thought. I don't smoke or drink, I'm practically a vegetarian, I exercise, I even wear sunscreen. Her analytical mind began to move through more and more questions. Why me? How did I get it? Why not me? she thought. It's just something of this world, and I'm just a normal person in the scheme of things.

Still tender from the biopsy, she slowly slid from behind the steering wheel. "Hi, Mom," Brian called, coming around the side of the house, then closing the car door for her. "Where've you been?"

A half-hour later Jim and Brent arrived home anxious to talk about the basketball practice. "What's Mom fixing for dinner tonight?" Brent asked, his stomach growling.

"I don't know, but I bet it's good," Jim said, pulling open the sliding glass door to the darkened kitchen. The familiar evening bustle—dinner on the stove, Brian doing homework or poking around for snacks—was absent. "Joan, we're home," he called, walking toward the den, their favorite room. On one wall hung the painting Joan's dad had done of the family farm with its white, five-sided barn and red roof, famous for stopping traffic back home in Iowa. In a corner was an ornate, ancient clock handed down from one generation to the next. On the mantle over a brick fireplace sat Jim's prized possession, a Central College game ball presented to him by the senior football players the year he and Joan had resigned and moved away. The ball was signed: "To our teacher, coach, and friend." The paneled room was quite unremarkable, but for them it was that safe haven where everyone piled on the sofa, spread out on the floor and played games, or wrestled.

It was there on the couch that Jim found Joan, talking to Brian. Both were in tears.

"Oh, Jim, it's cancer," she said the word softly, almost afraid to name it.

"Cancer?" Jim stared back at her. How could it be cancer? She was going for a routine check, he thought. "Cancer!" he repeated, as the shock from that single word washed over him. He had been hurrying around trying to catch up on a couple of reports at work—nothing crucial—while his wife was getting the worst news of her life. Crazy, disjointed thoughts ran through his mind. Cancer was associated with names in the obituaries. The tests had to be wrong. She was feeling so good, she was recovering . . . . He dropped to the couch, wrapping his arms around her as if to protect her from an invisible menace. Cancer! Had he misunderstood her phone call that morning? "I should have been with you," he mumbled the first thing that came to his mind.

"You didn't know. We didn't know. I thought the appointment was just to check the stitches," Joan said as Brent squeezed in beside her.

"I thought the doctor said all the tests were negative," Brian said angrily. Negative results—the best news possible—had been reported to him just last night when he returned with the church youth group from their ski trip. But the final tests had not come in.

"What's going to happen?" Brent asked worriedly, looking at each member of his family.

"We'll do whatever it takes to get rid of it, that's what," Joan told him, pulling him close. How good it felt to have her family around her. They would survive this by planning and keeping things as normal as possible, she vowed.

"Tell me again what the doctor told you," Jim asked, breaking into her thoughts. What he was hearing was so unbelievable that he needed to hear it all again.

"He said one last test showed traces of cancer, that a mastectomy was necessary," Joan said. "We have an appointment to discuss it tomorrow at his office."

"Tomorrow?"

"Yes, he wants to do the surgery in two days."

Somehow a supper no one had an appetite for was pulled together. Jim hated cooking, but preparing the meal at least gave him something to do. His mind returned to what Joan had told him. Traces of cancer—certainly not the news that they had hoped for but still, not terrible. "Traces is not bad," he began.

Joan caught his meaning immediately and rewarded him with a spirited smile. "At least they didn't say consumed with cancer—that is bad," she said. "Traces—we can deal with traces."

After dinner Jim insisted Joan rest on the couch. Brian took a phone call alerting the family that Brother Ben and Betty, his second wife, would arrive soon for a brief visit.

The boys helped clear the table and load the dishwasher while Jim scrubbed the pans. Cleaning up was the job he preferred, putting things in order so you could see you had accomplished something. He hurriedly dried the last skillet; he needed to call Joan's brother, Denny, before Ben arrived. He wanted to explain what was happening with Joan, then ask Denny to go the quarter-mile up the road to be with Joan's parents when he called them with the awful news.

Thankfully, the telephone remained silent and no visitors dropped by as the family grieved over this new diagnosis and began to make plans. It was important to be alone as a family, as each one began to deal with what Joan's cancer meant to them. From then on, each would be allowed to deal with it in his or her own way with support and understanding from the other family members.

"It's all set," Jim said hanging up the telephone. "Denny is going up to your folks' house to make sure they're okay when we call. He wondered if we had considered moving back to Iowa where we'd be close to the family."

Joan smiled at Denny's suggestion. It would be wonderful to be near her big brother but not practical. "I guess Denny forgot you have to work for a living. And besides, this won't last forever."

Once again the boys gathered around for a little while and they talked some more about moving, arriving once again at the conclusion that a move would not solve anything.

"Denny should be at your parents' house by now. Let's call and see if your folks can come back," Jim suggested.

Jim explained to Joan's folks what Joan had told him about the diagnosis and the surgery. Joan's dad agreed immediately that they would return to Hendersonville to take care of the boys and the house. He asked several more questions that neither Jim nor Joan was unable to answer before hanging up.

"It's so frustrating," Jim said, replacing the telephone. "We have such limited knowledge of what is going on or what these medical terms mean. It's hard to understand or explain any of it to someone else."

"We'll have more information tomorrow," Joan answered as the doorbell rang.

Brent bounded out of the kitchen. "I'll get it," he called, sliding toward the front door in his socks.

Ben and Betty stood at the door. Ben had visited in happier times—when they joined the church and as Brian prepared for confirmation. Here was someone who could understand what Jim was going through. From the pulpit, Ben had spoken openly of his first wife, Jerry, explaining what was happening with her and their family and emphasizing God's constant presence during Jerry's illness. As a parent, Jim knew Ben must have comforted his own two daughters when their mother was diagnosed with terminal cancer.

After saying a quick hello, both boys went to their rooms to be alone with their feelings.

"Cancer and death are not synonymous," Ben said, sitting down next to Joan as Betty settled into the recliner. Looking from Jim's strained face to Joan's, he began to calmly point out the positives that lay ahead.

"This is what you need to concentrate on, and this is what you need to be telling the boys. There are a number of things doctors can do to combat cancer. You'll have the best doctors and the best care," he said kindly. "God has a relationship to this in ways we don't understand. But we do know His love and power are there to help."

Ben's words brought Joan and Jim their first glimmer of hope. Everything seemed so strange to them just now, they did not know what to think. But Ben's words reassured them, gave them a basis for hope, and they clung to it.

Although Joan's cancer diagnosis came as a shock to Ben, he knew the church could bring God's love to this family through its actions just as it had for his family. He believed the church should provide a healthy concept of God so when difficult circumstances came along people did not hang their heads and say, "It is just God's will." Ben's presence there that evening suggested a willingness to support the Hendersons and to help them keep cancer and faith in perspective.

After asking permission from Joan and Jim, Ben spent a few minutes alone with each boy. Jim marveled at his minister's insight. He must have something important to tell them.

"It's okay to cry and to feel really bad because we understand it is painful inside," Ben said, sitting down on Brent's bed as the boy looked out at the black, winter sky. "But your mother is a real fighter and will really battle this thing, and she needs you to battle it with her. God doesn't want your mother to be sick. He doesn't cause the disease. God enters the picture in helping her fight the disease through the doctors and nurses and through the love of family and through His presence in ways that are sometimes difficult to understand."

Mindful that the family needed time alone together, Ben spoke briefly with Brian and then gathered the whole family for a prayer. "God cares very much for all of you," he reminded them as he and Betty prepared to leave. "I'll see you at the hospital Wednesday morning."

❖

In *The Sanctuary For Lent* Maxie Dunnam shares the word of an unknown writer:

> There is at least one useful and highly important task in this world that will not be done unless YOU do it.
>
> There will be someone with a breaking heart who will never have the courage to try again, unless YOU give it.
>
> There is some honest and righteous cause which needs just the additional support YOU can give it.
>
> There is some hard-pressed soul who will not get through the day of doubt unless, YOU pass along a simple word of encouragement.
>
> God has made you a necessity in some situation, and he has provided no substitute for YOU.

Members of First United Methodist were about to discover the truth in that writer's words. Similar to thousands of churches around the world, the church provides emotional and spiritual support through its fellowship. In other words, it provides God's love, present in human beings, reaching out to surround people with love. While committed caring did exist within the church, it was informal and largely unplanned, often carried out by a patient's Sunday school class or friends. No organized program was yet designed to assure smooth delivery of many of the services members provided.

One of the difficulties was an absence of training to prepare "helpers" to deal expertly with the patient and family in order to better provide what was needed. With a designated caring committee a system could be established to provide significant caring for all who were in need. Such a system could provide skill training to help eliminate missed opportunities for caring and could be built on a foundation that recognizes, develops, and then implements the God-given gifts of caring.

In *Called to Care*, Chester Custer writes, "Caring persons help us to keep the pieces of our lives together, but they also help us to experience as little loss as possible when our world seems to fall in around us. They help us to gain, or to regain perspective. They help us to see that all is not lost. They enable us to preserve, to consolidate, to rebuild. Caring persons appeal to our strengths." He goes on to say that the whole church, by its very nature, is to be a caring fellowship. "We dare not think of the caring ministry of the church as an optional function, as one of our alternatives, or as the concern simply of a few appointed persons."

Sometimes people assume that if no need is presented or is obvious, there is no need. Self-reliance and the pursuit of independence, while admirable, can rob people of the joy of interdependence. Lost is the feeling of being needed and valued through the sharing of gifts and resources. But providing for needs cannot occur in a vacuum, there must be a receiver.

Perhaps one of the greatest gifts is allowing others to share, therefore providing a climate for the discovery and development of individual talents. For how can one lead if no one will follow; give if no one receives; or show mercy and share heartache to a falsely cheerful countenance? When people open themselves to the love of others, it is not a matter of the strong giving to the weak, for both the giver and receiver are sharing their gifts.

Have you ever looked for a service in the Yellow Pages? If it is not listed or located where you think it should be, you believe it probably does not exist. Some people feel the same way about the services of the church. Look at the back of a Sunday bulletin or weekly newsletter. There is generally information about worship services, board meetings, recreational opportunities, and weekday school, but is there a local caring committee listed? Are any special groups of persons in the church trained to supplement home care services for persons who are chronically ill, incapacitated, or recuperating from an illness? An accessible caring group whose mission is identified and made known to the congregation allows persons in distress to feel comfortable when they ask for help. They are assured that they are connecting with a reliable source of help.

In *Support for Family Caregivers in the Community,* Susan Jacobs notes that by the year 2000 about seven million persons aged 65 or older will need help to remain at home. She goes on to list the daily stresses now faced by caregivers to the elderly and other homebound persons: physical strain of assisting the patient in activities of daily living; isolation and loneliness; loss of privacy and personal control of time; lack of sleep; emotional reaction to the physical decline and anticipated death of a loved one; expense, and family distress. Jacob says that caregivers, many with minimal or no additional support, may feel overwhelmed by the stress of caring for an older adult.

Other persons need help as they recover from surgery and treatment, or as they adjust to life with a disability. Churches often raise funds to pursue mission work away from the church and in other countries. Instituting a local care group would provide opportunities for church members to express concern and alleviate needs through social service at home.

Many families can benefit from the "comfort caregiver" concept described in an article in *Caring* magazine by Dawn T. Arrington and Karen S. Walborn. They write that "volunteer caregivers can provide "informal, temporary caregiving services that relieve families of constant caregiving duties."

Caring for chronically ill children with unpredictable futures can also be stressful and challenging. "The disruption caused by a chronic illness can lead to resentment. Family members may blame the client (ill member) for imposing on and disrupting 'normal' family life; often family members in turn feel guilty for having such resentment," write Diane Peters and Jamie Hills in *Caring.*

Results of a study begun in 1983 by the Cleveland diocese of the Catholic church indicated that rest or relief services for persons caring for incapacitated patients at home was generally unavailable. The study grew out of requests by the church's "friendly visitor" volunteers for more training. The volunteers were delivering increasing amounts of care while visiting.

Eventually respite programs developed by the diocese served 343 households for a total 11,876 hours. "Caregivers were frequently reluctant to use services of 'outsiders' even when they appeared to be in great need of a break," wrote Sr. Susan Klein in an issue of *Health Progress* magazine. "They often felt guilty if others helped care for an older relative. They were most likely to accept respite when a trusted person with an established relationship, such as their minister, recommended it. Highlighting the benefits of respite services to the incapacitated older adults and giving caregivers 'permission' to take a break so they could be renewed to continue giving care persuaded many caregivers to accept needed help."

A skyrocketing temperature, severe vomiting, uncontrollable pain—what happens and who helps when a crisis develops at home in the middle of the night and the patient must be taken to the hospital? How can parents keep things normal for their children when they are stressed by lack of sleep, escalating medical bills, and an uncertain future? Just knowing there is someone who cares, who wants to be called in a crisis, who will come day or night, can make a huge difference. For families with young children or the frail elderly, providing a middle of the night sitter in case of emergency will assure an easier rest for the caregiver or well spouse.

As the family works through their crisis, choosing hospitals, doctors, and treatment plans, people who can and will provide wholehearted support, reassurance, and availability can make their burden easier to bear.

❖

The Henderson home looked warm and inviting the night the family struggled to understand what cancer might mean to them. Brent's half-finished Lego building sat on the fireplace, Brian's school books were piled on a chair, a load of laundry hummed in the dryer. Anyone stopping in for a visit would have been met with a firm handshake, a friendly smile, and an optimistic outlook. Later, the family's courage in facing cancer and death one day at a time, living each moment as it came, was their gift to the community. Such a gift can make simple offerings seem insignificant, but they are not. Each act of caring reaffirms to the family that the community loves them and will stand by them, pushes back isolation and loneliness, and provides a sense of safety and belonging.

Joan seemed to be the archetype of those who survive cancer, and yet fear of the unknown gripped the whole family. The excitement of the window convention was already forgotten. All anyone could think about was the surgery scheduled for Wednesday.

❖ Three

The sun painted the morning sky a silvery blue with streaks of gold as Jim scraped frost from the windshield. He took no notice. In less than an hour, he and Joan would drive the seven miles to Hendersonville Hospital where Dr. Davis would perform a modified radical mastectomy, in an attempt to rid her of the cancer and determine how advanced the disease was. His heart felt dark and cold. A new sensation, a churning kind of sick fear, followed him wherever he went. It was impossible that he could lose her. First as a couple, then as a family, they were inseparable, skimming across the lake in their ski boat, floating lazily on rafts on Dale Hollow Lake, racing around on snowmobiles back in Iowa, or just sitting in the kitchen at night, sharing their day.

Why Joan? Why us? Why now? The randomness of cancer was crazy. Jerking open the car door, he jammed the key in the ignition, turned on the heater, and then slammed the door closed. "God, do you know what you're doing?" he demanded in the frosty silence. Back inside, he collected Joan's overnight case and called, "Time to go." Then he forced an encouraging smile as he helped Joan pull on her jacket.

At the traffic light next to their church, Jim watched a trickle of early morning commuters spill onto the Johnny Cash Parkway. Last week he had looked for familiar faces on the way to work. Today, illness made everything different. Other people were going on with their lives—to work and then home for dinner, to play, to enjoy their evening, to sleep in their own beds. How separate and removed he felt in the space of a few days of facing the unknown.

He circled Hendersonville Hospital, a three-story brick building on the edge of town. He stopped in front of the emergency room entrance used for early morning surgical patients, walked Joan inside, and then returned to park the car. They had rejoiced here just days earlier when preliminary reports showed no signs of cancer. Now, he wondered, would the mastectomy cure her? Was it already too late? No one knew.

Their life together had combined the shared excitement of careers blossoming and dreams coming true, the joy of a full, loving family life as best friends and best partners in life. Fear tightened its grip again as it had during the recent sleepless nights through which they held each other. The results of the coming surgery might untie the knot to all he held so dear.

Joan and Jim were welcomed by a nurse and shown to a small room where Joan changed into the hospital gown. The small room had a straight chair, a reclining chair, and a television.

"Nice outfit," Jim quipped, when Joan had slipped on the standard, blue, backless gown. He was rewarded with a smile.

Brought up in a world of fitness, Jim disliked hospitals. Being around sick people made him uncomfortable. He had recognized that inability to deal with illness early in his coaching career and usually assigned an assistant coach to take charge of injured players.

While Joan joked with the nurse who had come to give her a shot to make her drowsy, Jim pulled out his list of telephone numbers. Joan's folks would arrive the next afternoon. He would need to call Joan's brother, Denny, and a couple of friends when she came out of surgery. All of his appointments at work had been rescheduled, and his secretary knew where to reach him. The boys were at school.

While they waited, a doctor who was not a part of her surgeon's staff stopped in to talk. He had reviewed Joan's records, he told them, and agreed the surgery was necessary. The pace began to quicken as the anesthesiologist came to explain the IV he would use to put her to sleep. Someone else came and took her overnight case to her assigned room on the third floor. Then Brother Ben arrived, with a brief encouraging prayer. "Let's go," a green-smocked figure said, helping Joan onto the bed to transport her to surgery. Jim followed Joan as she was wheeled down the hall and into the elevator, then out again toward the operating rooms. "Slow down!" he wanted to shout. Instead he kissed Joan and promised to be there when it was over. Then he watched the doors to the surgery area, off limits to family, swing closed. There was no hint of her now, no security, no room.

❖

Jim turned and walked with Ben down the deserted, antiseptic-smelling hallway toward a miniature-sized waiting room where already a half-dozen people waited. He was glad Ben was with him. When he wanted to talk, Ben listened. When he wanted to be silent, Ben was silent. Ben was so comfortable to be with. Even so, Jim was beginning to feel the distance from home, from family and lifelong friends. Every other trauma in his marriage had been encountered as a couple or as a family. Now the boys were in school, Joan was in surgery, and he was alone, or so he thought.

Several Friendship Class members met Jim at the waiting room along with a handful of neighbors and friends. Their physical presence that day—even those who stayed only a few minutes—made it possible for Jim to reach out to them later. Beginning a list of visitors that day with their specific offers of help might have been beneficial later, but all thoughts were on Joan's surgery, not the recovery period.

Brooks shook Jim's hand, then walked with him down the hallway. A longtime class member, Brooks had been first welcomed into the class by Joan. He would make a habit during all of Joan's hospital stays to drop in on a regular basis, but just for five minutes or so.

When Brooks learned of the surgery, he felt moral support was all he could offer. Through the chronic illness and death of his own mother and other family members, he had learned that real friends show up when someone is sick or in trouble. He felt that if someone's sails were depleted, a short visit could puff them up again. He said to Jim, "I don't know exactly what you're going through, even though our circumstances may be similar. I understand there is not a lot I can do, but here I am. Let me know please, if there is something I can do."

Each time he came to the hospital, he said the same thing that he said to Jim that morning. "I don't want to get in your way. I just wanted you to know that I care about you, and I'm praying for you. If you need me, I'm here; otherwise, I'm gone."

Jim thanked him. He had been surprised to see Brooks, but glad he had stopped by.

Later, short visits gave Brooks time to assess the situation, one of his strong points, then make an offer of help. From experience he knew how quickly events could change in a hospital. He owned his own business and had a skill for problem solving. Loaded with nervous energy, he liked activity. If treatment was off schedule, he would offer to take Brent or Brian home; if Jim needed a sandwich, he would get it; if Jim needed to vent frustration with someone who could give him emotional support, Brooks stayed and walked the hall with him and listened. He knew that each individual has his or her own set of unique feelings toward life events, and he was willing to listen without judging.

As the morning dragged by, an unfamiliar couple introduced themselves, "We knew Joan's surgery was today and we just wanted to be here to let you know we are praying for you." Their words echoed the sentiments of others gathered there, people who needed to reach out and let Jim and Joan know they were not alone.

Most of the visitors knew one another and chatted among themselves as Jim paced the hallway with Ben. He was relieved when no one expected him to sit and talk. It was impossible to visit while surgeons looked for cancer in his wife. Knowing they cared was enough.

Suddenly, Doug, a longtime business associate and a member of Jim's Friday lunch bunch, appeared carrying a briefcase.

"It's okay, Doug, just go back to work," Jim told him after a brief greeting.

Doug shook his head. "Jim, this is important to me. I'm staying." Then pointing to his briefcase, he added, "I brought some work along; I'm just here. If you want to talk, fine, I'm here. But don't feel like you need to talk to me, I just want you to know that I really care, and I'm going to be here." And with that Doug walked down the hall, found a chair, snapped open his briefcase, and began to work.

Doug's a great friend, thought Jim. His appearance had validated their friendship. His words were exactly what Jim needed to hear. Doug had things to do to keep him busy, but if Jim needed him, Doug was there.

❖

Time seemed to stand still that morning, but at last the surgery was over. The arrival of Dr. Davis, still dressed in surgical green, in the waiting area stopped all conversations in mid-sentence. Joan was in recovery, the surgeon told Jim. The surgery had gone well, additional tests were being run, and the results would be back the next day. Decisions on additional treatment would be made based on those results. Another hour went by and at last the doors to the surgery unit swung open. The gurney carrying Joan was wheeled down the hallway on the way to her third floor room. Jim squeezed her outstretched hand as they rode the elevator upstairs.

He had been in Joan's room more than an hour when Barb and Diane knocked, then poked their heads in the door. "Go home," Diane told Jim, recognizing immediately he needed a break. He had been at the hospital all day and up in Joan's room for more than an hour. The two women were nearby neighbors of the Hendersons, and Diane worked part time as a nurse in the hospital emergency room. Jim was anxious to get home for a brief visit with Brian and Brent before returning to spend the night at the hospital. And yet, he did not want Joan to think he was abandoning her by leaving. Already he was beginning to feel the pull of needing to be in two places at once.

"Go! We will be here, we will sit here, we will stay here as long as you want us to stay," Diane said emphatically.

"Will you call me if there's any change?" Jim demanded.

"Yes," Barb said. "Now go. We'll take good care of her."

Joan was still groggy as Jim kissed her good-bye and promised to be back soon. Before leaving he rearranged her blankets, pulled them up under her chin, then looked doubtfully at Barb and Diane.

"She'll be fine with us," they told him.

As Barb and Diane sat quietly talking in a corner of Joan's small room, the intercom blared. "Code Red," said an official sounding voice.

"What's that?" the tall, sandy-haired Barb asked, jumping at the noise. The seriousness of her neighbor's condition had made her edgy.

"It's just a fire drill, it's not any big deal," Diane said calmly. In the hallway, the main unit doors slammed shut automatically, then each patient's room door was pulled shut by someone outside.

"Should we get Joan out of here?" Barb looked from Joan to the closed door, an uncomfortable feeling creeping over her. It was natural to defer to Diane, a short brunette who was at home in a hospital setting.

Diane shook her head. Opening a door closed during a fire drill was against all her training. She checked her watch and noted the time.

Five minutes went by, and the loud speaker crackled to life again. "Code Red Dietary. Code Red Dietary."

"I don't like this," Diane hissed to Barb. She did not want to alarm her friend, but Code Red Dietary meant there was a fire in the kitchen, and they were on the third floor, right over the kitchen.

"Diane, what's going on? You're making me nervous," Barb whispered.

"This is the real thing," Diane whispered back, going to the window. It would open only about eight inches, perhaps just enough for them to squeeze through if absolutely necessary.

"If that fire comes up here, how can we get Joan out this window onto the roof?" Diane wondered.

"Is this really serious?" Barb asked incredulously. Sometimes she could not tell when Diane was teasing.

Joan, listening quietly to all that was being said, propped one eye open and said in her firm, school teacher voice, "What's going on over there with you two?"

"No big deal, Joan," Diane said lightly, sounding every bit the unruffled nurse. "We're just standing over here looking out the window."

"What's all this stuff about a fire? Are you and Barb going out on the roof and leaving me in here alone?"

Barb and Diane looked at each other and then at Joan and grinned.

"No, no, no, Joan, we'll take you with us," Barb said sweetly, as if speaking to a two-year-old.

Diane, thinking she smelled smoke, went over to the door and felt it to see if it was warm. The sound of sirens was getting louder as the fire trucks came up the road next to the hospital. "This door isn't hot yet," she said. "But when it gets hot, we're all three going out the window. We'll put the IV pole out the window on the roof, and Barb can hold it. Then we'll put you on your side, you just get real stiff, and I'll pass you out to Barb."

All three looked at each other and burst into laughter until tears ran down their faces. There was no way any of them could have gotten out the window, but planning a daring escape made them a team, and for a few minutes thoughts of the future evaporated. Out of all the bad that was happening, it was still good to be together, and to laugh. Thirty minutes later a "Code Clear" announced the emergency was over, and Barb went out to find out what was happening.

Diane went to Joan's bedside to check her pulse. "I know this is serious," Joan told Diane, almost as if she was beginning to sense what lay ahead for her. Joan had never really been sick since moving to Hendersonville. Now her neighbor was sitting with her, nursing her. Roles were changing, her world was being shaken. She had always been the strong one—cleaning wounds, taking kids to the emergency room—now it was her turn to be taken care of.

"Joan, you may not be ready to talk now, but I'm ready to listen whenever you're ready," Diane answered. "I can handle whatever you say, and we can cry together."

Later, on the way home, Barb and Diane discussed who would be the most logical person to spend the night with Joan. They agreed that after supper they would return, and if Joan were doing well, Barb would stay. If not, Diane, with her nursing experience, would take over. When they returned to the hospital, Jim was seated on Joan's bed. When they announced their plan, Joan rolled her eyes and explained she had other ideas. "I'm still in control," she said with a laugh. "No one is staying. I'm tired and need to get some sleep!"

❖

On Thursday morning when Barb popped in for a visit, the room was somber. "We didn't get the news we wanted," Joan told her, obviously shaken. "Preliminary reports show more cancer."

Before Barb could speak, Joan's weary features were transformed into a huge smile.

"Denny!" Joan gasped in disbelief, looking past Barb.

Joan's brother, his skin weathered from years of work on the farm, filled up the doorway with his six-foot, five-inch frame. "Hi, Sis," he said softly.

Jim's spirits soared too with his brother-in-law's unexpected arrival. They had always had a close relationship and having him here now was the one bright spot in a horrible week.

After gently embracing Joan, Denny quickly explained he had flown into Nashville, then taken a taxi to the hospital.

"Denny, this is . . . ." Joan was so shaken she could not remember her longtime friend's name.

Barb, realizing this was family time, introduced herself, then quickly departed.

"You didn't tell me you were coming," Jim said, seizing Denny in a hug. They had spoken just hours earlier when Jim called Denny's Iowa farm home. In the coming days, just having Denny there, someone he could express any emotion to without having to be careful or on his guard, would help Jim get through the awful first days of Joan's diagnosis. Swearing or questioning God about Joan's cancer was something Jim was not too anxious to do around most of his friends. Here, in Denny, was someone who would understand. Someone who deeply loved Joan.

Denny and Joan had always had a "If you need me, I'm there" kind of relationship—big brother, caring sister. His arrival transformed her from an exhausted patient to a spunky little sister anxious to get home.

Denny had not waited for a final diagnosis. If the surgeons had removed all the cancer, he would be there for the greatest celebration the family ever held. And, if the news was bad—well, going through the worst of times, both Jim and Joan needed to be surrounded by those who really cared.

To Jim, Denny's flight to Tennessee substantiated his membership in the group that really cared. Others too would move in and out of that group by their words and actions.

For Brian and Brent, Uncle Denny's unexpected arrival at their home that evening restored some balance. They did not talk much about the cancer. Instead, he took them out to eat, out for an ice cream, and a ride. They were just two kids with a special uncle, and with all the upset and uncertainty, it felt good just to be together.

All during the day on Thursday, Joan's room began to fill with flowers and plants. A plant in a football-shaped container was sent home for Brian and Brent to enjoy. Several persons, not wanting to disturb Joan, left cards at the hospital reception desk. Under orders to purchase a plant from his Friday lunch bunch, Doug had walked into a local floral shop and told the florist, "Give me the biggest thing you have."

Now it was sitting in Joan's room, all six feet of it, practically attacking visitors. "Really nice, I have to pay for another private room to house this stupid plant," she joked, obviously pleased with his gesture. "Doesn't Doug know how to pick out flowers for a hospital room?"

Joan's parents flew in that evening, going straight to the hospital to await the doctor's visit with Denny, Joan, and Jim. Things were being brought under control as Joan's caring family surrounded her and Jim and the boys with love and support.

A groundwork of support had been laid by the Friendship Class the day of Joan's surgery. Specific offers of food, childcare, and transportation had been made. Jim had taped notes and cards from several persons offering a ride or some other help to the inside of a kitchen cupboard door over the telephone—just in case.

That night Joan and Jim asked Denny to stay with them when the surgeon came to discuss Joan's test results. When he arrived, their family doctor and another man were with him. Joan's parents waited in the hallway.

"We got the test results back, and we need to talk about them," Dr. Davis said, explaining there were signs of cancer in her system. He introduced Dr. Fernando Miranda, an oncologist (cancer doctor) at nearby Nashville Memorial Hospital's Cancer Center, and asked him to take over and explain what that meant.

Dr. Miranda nodded his approval of Denny's presence. Instinctively this family was already doing the right thing—including a third party in conversations with physicians. About ninety percent of what he told Joan and her family would be quickly forgotten, but someone with a cool head, preferably uninvolved, would remember details and explain them later.

Both Jim and Denny strained to hear and understand everything the oncologist was telling them. Later when they tried to tell Joan's parents what they had heard, they could only agree that Joan's cancer was serious and that chemotherapy would start soon. However, the particulars were fuzzy, as if they had heard two different versions of the same story.

"We use a lymph node count as an elementary measure of what treatments are necessary," Dr. Miranda explained. "If little or no cancer is in the lymph nodes, we use chemotherapy as insurance. If a medium cancer count is present in the nodes, then there is a strong recommendation for chemotherapy."

Jim, filled with dread, gripped Joan's hand and waited for the doctor to continue. He could not look at her. "In Mrs. Henderson's case, there is a high count. Tests show one of the most common cancers of the breast, infiltrating ductal adenocarcinoma," Dr. Miranda said. "The tumor, a portion of which could not be removed, grew to one inch in diameter in about three weeks, indicating we're dealing with an invasive, fast-moving cancer."

As he outlined treatment plans, he was careful not to discourage the family, but he wanted to make them know how critical the situation was. "We'll give you as much chemotherapy as we can as fast as we can," he said.

Cancer chemotherapy is a chemical treatment which disrupts cancer cells' ability to grow and multiply. A combination of drugs, given at home, in a doctor's office, in a hospital, or in a clinic is delivered either orally, intravenously, or by injection depending on the type of cancer, the stage of development, and the health of the patient. Cost of the chemotherapy and length of treatment vary according to individual needs.

"The first thing is to accept the disease, get a knowledge of it, continue a normal life, and cut down on stresses," the oncologist advised them.

Joan and Jim wanted more information but at first they were too dazed to even formulate questions. So much of the language of cancer and its treatment was new to them. Instead of nodding in blank agreement, they asked Dr. Miranda to explain again what the cancer meant and what the treatment would mean.

Very quickly, Dr. Miranda sensed Joan would not be a typical patient who refused to accept the diagnosis or who allowed him to direct the treatment without question. Though she was still shocked by the cancer diagnosis and the need for a year of treatment, she was already beginning to take hold of her disease, accepting it and preparing to face it head-on.

He knew she would do better in treatment because her attitude was so positive and so was her husband's. Through years of providing treatment, Dr. Miranda had discovered that the spouse of a cancer patient plays a big role in how a person will fight cancer. Many weak moments would occur throughout Joan's treatment and Jim must be there to support her.

Already he could see Joan would be more like a partner than a patient in her upcoming treatment. Together they began to make decisions about treatment which was to begin in five days. Joan insisted she be given the first chemotherapy treatment as an outpatient so she could stay home with her children.

The physician agreed, although with the strength of the drugs she would be given most people needed to be hospitalized. But, he warned her, if she or the family could not handle the side effects she would have to be admitted.

For Joan and Jim, this was a first lesson in "You can get, if you ask."

Hard, frightened tears flowed when at last the doctors, Denny, and Joan's parents had gone. Joan and Jim needed to spend time together without visitors, to grieve for the future that seemed to have been snatched away and replaced with a kaleidoscope of uncertainties—from life itself to reactions to treatment to maintaining a normal life for the children. Joan had the solace of knowing Jim would stand by her. Just that morning he had offered to help her with her bath. Her nurse had been surprised. "You sure you don't want me to do this," she had asked. But Jim had wanted to get it behind them. It was his way of saying the mastectomy was okay, that it did not change his love for her.

Joan had laughed when Jim quipped, "No, I'll do it. We've been doing this for years."

She had once written in a diary, "Ecclesiastes 4:9-12 describes Jim and me," and again that morning she had known it was true.

> Two can accomplish more than twice as much as one, for the results can be much better. If one falls, the other pulls him up; but if a man falls when he is alone, he's in trouble. Also, on a cold night, two under the same blanket gain warmth from each other, but how can one be warm alone: And one standing alone can be attacked and defeated, but two can stand back-to-back and conquer; three is even better, for a triple-braided cord is not easily broken (*AP*).

"I thought if I just had the mastectomy it would be okay," Joan said, wiping her eyes. Already she had forgotten the name of the cancer, but the words her doctor used to describe it seemed burned into her mind. "The cancer is like a million pin dots. It's unusual, tricky, very aggressive, and usually fatal."

Joan did not even consider dying of the cancer. She was going to make it! Cancer was a temporary inconvenience. She had so much she wanted to do with Jim and with Brian and Brent, a whole life to live.

People had told Jim that waiting for the diagnosis was the worst part of an illness. In the moments after the oncologist explained the seriousness of Joan's condition, Jim knew that was not true. Knowing was the worst. The hope that he and Joan had was gone. Now they had to work at finding new hope. Jim got up and rearranged the flowers that lined the window sill.

"What will you tell the boys?" Joan asked, watching him.

"We'll tell them the way it is, what the doctors told us," Jim answered. "That it's really serious, that you'll have chemotherapy . . . ."

"Tell them the doctors are really good and we feel everything will be okay," Joan said. "They may not like what we are saying, but we've got to tell them the truth."

❖

For a support group that is already organized, the time when a diagnosis has been made and a treatment plan has been designed is the time that the family can reflect over offers of help as they begin to learn about treatments, therapies, and long-term prognosis. The listing of specific services will help distressed persons know that the entire family unit has access to help.

A 1987 booklet from the US Department of Health and Human Services reports that in a 1984 study of initial responses to a cancer diagnosis by 340 patients, twenty-nine per cent indicated shock, fear, and disbelief; twenty-seven per cent had a positive attitude; sixteen per cent felt angry, depressed, or hopeless; nine per cent did not want to think about it; seven per cent saw an amputated future; six per cent experienced renewed faith; and six per cent felt doomed. Many of the respondents noted multiple reactions. "The study repeatedly showed that physical comfort (such as hand holding) helped dissipate the panic and fear these people said they experienced. Talking to them, offering encouragement and support resulted in the cancer patient being able to adopt a positive attitude and determination to conquer the disease."

The researchers concluded that those who react most positively use a knowledge of the disease to beat the cancer. "Those who react with fear, panic, anxiety, and hopelessness need physical comfort, support, realistic hope, encouragement, and the physical presence of others."

There are varying types of mastectomies, ranging from removal of soft breast tissue to removal of soft tissue and some muscle to removal of soft tissue, muscle to the surface of the bone, and some or all the lymph tissue from beneath the armpit. Length of recovery, loss of strength to arms and hands, and amount of pain vary depending on the extent of the surgery. To accurately say "I know how you feel" about another's mastectomy is impossible.

❖

Joan's surgeon cut away breast tissue and lymph glands from a 32-square-inch area but on Sunday she was up, had taken a bath, and was eagerly planning to talk to Dr. Davis about going home. Neither she nor Jim was too concerned about chemotherapy. They had already made up their minds that by gathering plenty of information, setting specific, attainable goals, and hanging onto a positive attitude she would do just fine. If anyone could beat this thing called cancer, it would be Joan.

Casual friends, also members of their church, dropped in after services on Sunday, the first persons aside from regular friends to come visit. "We're just really concerned and wanted you to know that we care. Is there anything we can do?" they asked. They had heard reports of Joan's surgery and diagnosis at church and remarked with surprise that Joan was already up and around. Then, instead of bombarding Joan and Jim with questions or relating other cancer stories, they allowed Jim to take the lead and simply listened.

By then, the initial shock that the cancer was not gone had worn off. There had been time to grieve and to make plans. Both Jim and Joan were comfortable sharing with the couple parts of what the doctor had told them and plans for treatment.

After about ten minutes, the couple again offered their assistance and stood up to leave. "We're fine, Joan's folks are here, the boys are taken care of, and she has just one chemotherapy treatment every third Friday," Jim said with conviction as he walked them to the elevator. "We even have cancer insurance."

Henri Nouwen writes in *Out of Solitude*, "When we honestly ask ourselves which persons in our lives mean the most to us, we often find that it is those who, instead of giving much advice, solutions or cures, have chosen rather to share our pain and touch our wounds with a gentle and tender hand. The friend who can be silent with us in a moment of despair or confusion, who can stay with us in an hour of grief and bereavement, who can tolerate not-knowing, not-curing, not-healing and face with us the reality of our powerlessness, that is the friend who cares."

Joan's and Jim's spirits were buoyed by their hospital visitors who stayed brief periods of time and whose interest allowed them to talk about upcoming treatment and concerns. In addition, Jim's Uncle John began to telephone on a regular basis. Jim knew that Uncle John could identify with him since his own wife had died from breast cancer many years earlier. Although she had been through major surgery and they both knew that a major battle with cancer was looming just ahead, at that moment, she was getting better, not worse.

Joan and Jim were beginning a journey. They did not know how long it would last or what perils and pitfalls were along the way. But they did know when they had needed them most, their friends and acquaintances had shown up, made offers to help, and made themselves and their concern known. Just talking with others had eased some of the anxiety. They did not expect to need any help, but knowing others were concerned felt good. In a few days, both the treatment and the getting well would be underway. Joan already was feeling better and tomorrow she would be home.

❖ *Four*

"Nice letter," Jim said, laying the single sheet of stationery on Joan's hospital bed. Four days had passed since the surgery. Joan was now dressed and packing her gowns, letters, and cards in her overnight case preparing to go home.

The letter was from Diana Diaz, a member of the Friendship Class, who was well-known in the church and community for her work with the American Cancer Society. Her involvement was a natural outgrowth of her chosen field, oncology nursing. Diana took her turn teaching the class and attended class work projects and parties whenever she could. Her aggressive take-charge attitude guaranteed that anything she took on would be done well.

A close friend had recently died of cancer and Diana had found that offering to help was difficult. But she soon decided Joan's cancer was something she could not ignore. She had delivered an upbeat letter to the hospital telling Joan she had seen many people survive cancer, and if anyone would give it a good run, she knew that Joan would. In her letter she reminded the Hendersons of her cancer nursing background and offered whatever help the family needed.

Joan was especially touched by Diana's letter. "Diana is so busy. She has a young son, and besides nursing at the hospital, she also teaches and is working with her husband while he starts up his practice," she told Jim, snapping her suitcase shut with one hand. Her left arm was held close to her chest, and for the time being, she was unable to use it.

"Should we bother her?" Jim wondered. The letter came at a critical time with chemotherapy scheduled at the end of the week. They had limited information about treatment and wanted more up-to-date reading material.

Joan sat on the bed and glanced over the letter again. "It sounds like she wants to help. Will you call her?"

Jim found a phone book in the bedside cabinet, located Diana's number and dialed. Diana agreed to come to their home Monday night after Joan was discharged from the hospital. Their confidence in her and willingness to ask for information made her feel good. She had trained for years to work with cancer patients. Helping a friend by using all the knowledge she had made Diana feel that at least she was doing something constructive for the Hendersons.

❖

Even as a young child Joan understood the connection between following instructions and doing a good job. Both adventuresome and fearless, she loved to ride behind her father on horseback as he worked the cattle. When she was older, she drove the tractor as her father, brother, and cousins baled hay for the cattle. Worried at first that the tractor would roll backward on the hills, Joan paid careful attention to her father's instructions and became his best driver, taking over her grandfather's job of plowing in the field the spring after he died.

While at college, Joan worked as a resident advisor in a freshmen women's dorm where her ability to listen and solve problems smoothed out dorm life for younger students. Then, while working for Ron Schipper, the Central College football coach, she observed and admired his organizational skills. His football drills were timed to the second, and his itineraries for team trips were so highly organized they were scheduled down to the minute.

Schipper, one of the nation's winningest football coaches, believed organization was the key to success. "You're not any smarter, your team members aren't going to be any better. The only thing you can do is out-organize the others. By organization you can build a program that builds on itself."

Throughout her life Joan believed in learning all she could, then doing the best that she could. Organization helped her do that. Learning all about cancer, then doing the best she could with what she learned, seemed a natural thing to do. The percentages of those who

survived her type of cancer were not really very important to her or
Jim. If there was only one survivor out of a hundred, they knew she
would be the one, because together they planned to out-organize their
opponent.

That meant preparing for the fight—learning how to decrease
stress, planning for good nutrition, setting priorities, getting enough
rest, avoiding people while her blood counts were low, and staying
involved with life. Difficult instructions even for someone who is well
and loaded with energy. And each item on the list seemed a
contradiction. Good nutrition meant shopping at the grocery store and
preparing food. Shopping was a double whammy—being around
people with germs and using precious energy, both of which increased
stress. Stress brought on lack of sleep, creating an environment for
short tempers and frustration. It would be a downward vicious cycle
without help—but right now Joan was feeling so good she was not too
concerned. At times, in fact, she felt so good that she and Jim wondered
if she had been diagnosed correctly. She could cook, Jim could do the
grocery shopping, and she could take a nap while the boys were at
school.

❖

When Diana arrived at the Henderson home after dinner Monday
night, she said candidly, "I can't emotionally do this unless I just do it
the way I do for people that I don't even know."

After a quick introduction to Joan's mom and dad who were busy
in the kitchen, Joan and Jim led Diana into the living room where she
could spread out her materials. Diana produced a set of flip charts that
helped explain what they could expect during chemotherapy. Already
tears were welling up in her eyes so she warned them, "I'm probably
going to cry, so just let me run through this."

In addition to being in the same Sunday school class, Diana and
Joan both played in the church bell choir. Although there was ten years
difference in their ages, the two enjoyed throwing witticisms back and
forth along with the rest of the bell ringers, but they had not socialized

outside church activities. Still, telling Joan what treatment would be like was one of the most difficult things Diana had ever done.

Since Joan did not know which drugs she would take during her first treatment on Friday, Diana discussed chemotherapy in general and the possible side effects—hair loss, vomiting, constipation, fever, bleeding, bruising, nosebleeds, and mouth sores.

Other more drug specific side effects were listed in *Chemotherapy and You: A Guide to Self-help and Treatment*, a book Diana planned to leave with Joan. Skin damage, joint pain, dizziness, mental depression, numbness, irregular heartbeat, chest pain, rapid heartbeat, and sensitivity to sunlight were all possible. Some of the side effects were quite rare whereas other reactions were more common.

"This is how some people react." Diana told them. "And, you may really, really feel crummy, and you may feel indescribably weary."

Eventually Joan would suffer almost every side effect Diana talked about and those listed in the book. Once the chemotherapy began and her energy levels began to hit bottom, even getting up to get a glass of water became a major decision. Her fatigue became so extreme that dragging herself to the den to spend time with the family was impossible, even though she longed to just lie on the couch and watch them.

Right then, though, Joan's biggest concern was losing her hair; it seemed so strange to think of herself bald. "I hate to think about losing my hair. Isn't there something they can do about that?" Joan asked, running her fingers through her wavy, brown hair.

Diana nodded, it was a natural concern. "They'll probably wrap your head in ice," she said. "Sometimes that keeps the hair from falling out. There are other serious side effects with chemotherapy, but remember there are drugs that can combat those things." As she explained basic mouth care and infection control for chemotherapy patients, Diana began to realize that the Hendersons, much like others she had worked with, looked at Joan only in her present state—she was not bruising, her mouth was in good shape, she had energy—and it was making it difficult to identify with the information she gave them that they would need later.

Diana took out a green spiral notebook. "I want to show you where to find all the information I'm giving you—just in case you need it."

She gave them the copy of *Chemotherapy and You*. Written in plain English, the book was well organized and specific information was easy to find. It included sample questions that one may use when talking with doctors about chemotherapy. "Medicines affect people differently," Diana explained. "Friends may recognize the name of one of your drugs and assume you will have a reaction identical to theirs. But everyone is different."

Turning to the section on questions to ask about chemotherapy, Diana strongly encouraged both Joan and Jim to stay as informed as they could. "Make sure your information is coming from a good source. You may get conflicting information. If you are, say, 'Dr. X said this, why are you differing?' Or, 'I've gotten two different pieces of information about that, let me see if I can clear this up.' Remember, you're dealing with your life. Don't ever think a question is stupid. Get a telephone number to call both day and night for questions that won't wait. Find out what side effects you should report immediately, and follow the doctor's recommendations on foods to avoid and instructions on taking other medications."

When she had finished answering questions, Diana packed up her charts, and then went to say good-bye to Joan's parents. She was glad they had come; Joan would need all the help she could get.

"Thanks for coming," Jim said, walking Diana to her car.

Driving home, Diana breathed a heavy sigh, thankful she had gone.

Not everyone will have friends who are medical professionals to turn to when their illness is diagnosed. But even then, instead of guessing about what the patient should do, supporters can help by offering to make lists of questions for the patient to ask the doctor. Learning about the disease with your friends, talking with them about their treatment, and staying in touch with their needs keeps communication lines open and decreases the likelihood of misinformation.

❖

Cheryl Dismukes was the third nurse friend to offer her special skills to Joan and Jim. Cheryl's husband, John, had been expecting a call from Jim, but not about cancer. The men had coached their sons' baseball team the previous year, and now it was time to begin planning for the upcoming season. When the two men talked earlier in the week, Jim had passed along the good news that Joan's biopsy had been clear. Now Jim was telling him that Joan had cancer and that thirteen of the eighteen lymph nodes the doctor had removed also were cancerous.

After extending his sympathies and offering whatever assistance Jim might need, John hung up and went straight to the kitchen where Cheryl was preparing lunch. She worked as a quality assurance nurse at nearby Nashville Memorial Hospital, and she would know how serious Joan's condition was.

"That was Jim Henderson," John said. "Joan had surgery Wednesday. They removed eighteen lymph nodes and thirteen of them are cancerous. What does that mean?"

Cheryl's face went white, her bubbly mood evaporated. "She's living every woman's nightmare," she told John. Stunned by the news, Cheryl dabbed at her eyes with a tissue and then sat down stiffly at the table. She and Joan had volunteered to staff a refreshment stand at summer concerts to raise funds for their sons' ball field. Their lively personalities had meshed and they became friends. They attended different churches and both had stayed so busy they had not seen each other since the baseball season. Cheryl remembered all the times Joan had rubbed on sunscreen at ball games and slipped on sunglasses to protect her eyes from cataracts. "It's so unfair!" Cheryl cried as the severity of the news sunk in.

Nursing was an important part of Cheryl's life. While she had worked toward her nursing degree, a neighbor with four children of her own kept Cheryl's and John's two children without pay. "Just pass it on," Cheryl's friend told her. Now was her chance, but where did she start?

We're at the same stage in life, Cheryl thought, identifying with Joan's situation. We want healthy, happy children. We want to see our children start their families. As a nurse she knew the score and that Joan could not afford a mistake, the product of any one's error, or anything else that would deviate from an intense, consistent fight against her cancer.

As Joan and Jim tried to come to grips with news of the cancer and how best to prepare to fight the disease, Cheryl felt God leading her to help Joan. However, she resisted calling or visiting Joan and Jim for fear that she would cry in front of them.

By Monday Cheryl was thoroughly miserable. "I'm afraid to go see her. I'm afraid my being upset will cause Joan to become upset," she told her co-workers at the hospital. Still, she wanted and needed to do something.

"Cheryl, you can't lie and tell her everything is going to be okay. All you have to say is, 'I'm sorry,' " an oncology floor nurse told her. "Go to her. You'll feel better and so will she."

That night before leaving her office, Cheryl gathered several pamphlets about cancer to take to Joan, but when she arrived at Hendersonville Hospital to deliver them, Joan had already been discharged. "Home free," she sighed, getting back on the elevator. That evening she paged through one of the pamphlets, *Taking Time: Support for People with Cancer and the People Who Care About Them*. The book had reinforced her conviction that the emotional well-being of the whole Henderson family was under siege. When one member is ill, others in the family must assume new roles. From her work at the hospital she knew the entire family faced upheaval and readjustment with Joan's cancer, not just Joan. Cheryl called a family conference.

When her husband and children had gathered at the kitchen table, Cheryl explained she wanted to help Joan in any way possible, if they all agreed. Just reading about what the needs of the family were during a lengthy illness made her want to help. She could only imagine what life would be like for her own children, Jennifer and Chris, if she were in Joan's place. "There is so much fear of the unknown going into cancer treatment. Maybe my crazy personality will help her deal with the crises she'll face," Cheryl shared with her family. "But I'll need your support. Can I count on it?"

"Let's do it," John said with firm resolve.

"Be there," Chris, their fourteen-year-old son volunteered with youthful concern and enthusiasm. Mrs. Henderson was the mother of a friend. He wanted his mother to help in any way she could.

Jennifer nodded her head. "Call her, Mom," she urged.

Cheryl walked to the telephone hesitantly but with purpose and dialed the Hendersons' number. When Jim answered she told him, "Jim, I want you to know I'll do whatever I can do to help, whatever you want. I know the ropes at the hospital, perhaps I can make it easier."

Jim seized the opportunity to ask Cheryl to meet with them the next night and talk about cancer treatment. After talking with Diana earlier that evening, he and Joan were anxious to get every piece of knowledge about cancer they could. Besides, Cheryl worked at Nashville Memorial, the hospital where the chemotherapy would be administered. They were unfamiliar with the hospital and could get some insight about it from her.

When she had finished speaking with Jim, Cheryl dialed Julie, her pastor's wife, who was developing a local hospice, a program that offers medical and bereavement care to terminally ill patients and their families. She explained her plan to Julie to commit to go to each chemotherapy treatment with Joan.

Julie listened thoughtfully as Cheryl told what was happening with Joan. She then gave Cheryl a very special gift. "Cheryl, if the time comes that you need me to come and do what you're doing for Joan and Jim, I will," she said. "Don't ever think of yourself as a failure because you don't have anything left to give. It's perfectly normal for immediate caregivers to get maxed out."

Cheryl, strong with commitment, did not realize the importance of those words. But, as the months went on, that bit of insight from Julie and her offer of help became the most important gift Cheryl could receive during the time she spent helping the Hendersons.

The next night Cheryl and John delivered the chemotherapy books to the Hendersons, and Cheryl made her offer to ride to Joan's chemotherapy treatment on Friday.

"No, really Cheryl, we'll be okay. You don't have to put yourself out," Jim said, while Joan nodded agreement with him. The last thing they wanted was to be a burden.

"Jim, I really want to do this," Cheryl said firmly, standing her ground. "I'll meet you in your church parking lot, and we can ride over and back together. You may need someone with you to help Joan. In the meantime, I'll go over to the cancer center and find out their check-in procedures so we'll know what to do Friday."

❖

By nature, Jim and Joan were well-informed, methodical people who planned constantly. Talking with both Cheryl and Diana underscored their conviction that becoming informed as much as possible about Joan's treatments was vitally important.

Paging through a copy of *Love, Medicine & Miracles* by Bernie Siegel, M.D. (a gift from their associate pastors and recommended by Cheryl) further reinforced that their quest for information was valid. "This is a book about surviving and about characteristics that survivors have in common," the book jacket read. "It is about healing and about how exceptional patients can take control in order to heal themselves. It is about courage—about patients who have the courage to work with their doctors to participate in and influence the course of their illness."

While that book and others like it were helpful, as were some suggestions from well-meaning friends, the family had to guard against unrealistic expectations by friends, relatives, and even in the literature they read. Some of what they read and heard made it seem that if they just prayed enough, if Joan just tried hard enough, if they just had the right attitude, she could beat the cancer.

Exasperated with those types of comments, Joan finally had to say to a beloved friend, "You can't do this to me. I'm trying as hard as I can, and if I don't make it, you're making it seem like I didn't try."

For Joan and Jim, people who simply recognized a need, even a small one, and quietly filled it became the mainstay of their support. The many gifts of caring ultimately became a huge gift. The extravagant gestures were not the ones that made the difference, it was individuals doing the one thing they enjoyed doing—an artist painting a hat, a seamstress making a dress, a teenager baking a batch of cookies, and out-of-town friends making contact. And it was others saying hello instead of ducking out of sight in the grocery store to avoid contact.

The opportunity to share their concerns and questions with three very assertive nurses, Diana, Cheryl, and Diane, who in turn coached them on the best use of the medical field, helped Joan and Jim become the informed consumers of medical services they needed to be. All three agreed with Joan when she told them, "I don't want to be at the doctor's mercy. I am still in charge of my life, no matter how limited that may be."

"Realize that your medical care is a service, a very expensive service. Just like getting carpet laid," Diane told Joan as they sipped tea in Joan's kitchen. "If you don't understand what the carpet layer is telling you, you ask questions. This is your life. If you don't understand what the doctor is telling you, ask questions. While you're relaxing or getting ready to fall asleep, questions will pop into your head, so keep paper and pencil nearby. Ask your doctor to write down the name of the person he wants you to direct questions to if he is not available. You can also ask the nurse who is giving you the treatment to give you information."

Part of being in charge was making sure in their own minds that Joan was getting the very best treatment for her type of cancer. Therefore, Jim had Joan's records sent to a medical institute in Houston known for its cancer treatment. The response was exactly what was hoped for. "Treatment at Nashville Memorial is what we recommend based on the diagnosis," the letter from the institute said, confirming Dr. Miranda's treatment plan.

Although Joan was getting lots of practical information, a visit from a member of the church also answered many of her questions. Shirley had been introduced to Joan by her daughter-in-law several years earlier. She too had undergone a mastectomy and chemotherapy. She had also been trained as a volunteer for the American Cancer Society's *Reach To Recovery* program, a group of women who have had mastectomies and who share their insights and experiences with other women.

Shirley could tell Joan what kind of brassiere to purchase, and where to go to purchase a prosthesis. "Wear a sweater to make certain it looks right," she advised Joan.

Then Joan was ready for more difficult information. "Shirley, I know I have a fast-growing kind of cancer. I know it will be an uphill battle. Did you have any lymph nodes with cancer in them?" she asked, hungry for someone who had the same circumstances and had done well.

Shirley was honest. "Just one," she told Joan. Then she added, "But a woman I know through *Reach To Recovery* had cancer in numerous lymph nodes, and she's still living."

As they talked about Shirley's personal experience with chemotherapy, Shirley was able to share the physical and emotional effect it had on her. "Joan, it throws the body into an unnatural state— havoc! Don't hold your emotions back. If you feel like crying, cry! If you can't sleep, ask for medication to calm down. And seek professional help if you can't do it alone," she said kindly.

Shirley kept in touch with Joan weekly by sending cards that said, "I'm thinking of you." The cards reminded Joan that Shirley was there if she needed her and was pulling for her. "Any questions, just call," she wrote. In turn, Joan, a woman who kept her faith when it was tested, became a positive force in Shirley's life.

Later, Joan began to call newly-diagnosed cancer patients to encourage them and to provide personal insight just as Shirley and others had done for her.

❖

The First United Methodist bell choir room was filled with an air of expectancy as members took their places before long tables lined with bells. The group, on the way to becoming friends as they struggled to learn new music, was awaiting the arrival of Joan's bell partner, Marilynn. Joan was already at her place, waiting.

Marilynn raced up the steps, late as usual, then stopped at the door to the choir room, astounded. There sat Joan, one week after her mastectomy, looking pleased with herself. "I don't believe this!"

Marilynn said finally, shaking her head as she rushed to greet Joan. The two were a likely pair and the source of many bell choir jokes—playing sharps when flats were called for, running out of music to play before a song was over, and even playing the wrong music in church while the rest of the choir tried to get their attention.

"I can't believe you're here!" Marilynn said again, reaching out to hug her friend.

Joan held up a hand in a warm warning, "Careful, I'm delicate, you know."

"Are you playing or watching?" their director asked.

"Playing," Joan said, "but just one bell."

"I suppose you expect me to pick up the slack," Cheryl R., who stood on Joan's other side, teased.

"Uh-huh," Joan and Marilynn said in unison.

Joan played the whole hour seated on a red cushioned stool as jokes flew. Sitting between Marilynn and Cheryl R., ringing one bell, she could feel their love and support surrounding her. It felt great to be back. Such little things brought greater pleasure than ever.

When practice was over, someone asked what was next for her and Joan explained her planned treatment for the next year. She was to undergo chemotherapy for thirty weeks, then radiation for five weeks. "There are lots of lovely side effects, like no hair, numbness, and nausea, so I can't be held accountable for my bell playing," she said, keeping things light.

"Okay, that's your excuse, what will Marilynn's be?" quipped someone.

"She's my bell partner, what more excuse do I need?" Marilynn joined in, helping Joan with her coat.

Diana, also a member of the bell choir, nodded her approval. It was good for Joan to be sharing some of what was happening to her so friends could get an accurate idea of what Joan was going through— except she made everything sound so simple and easy.

"I can't believe you're out with all that treatment coming up," someone said.

Joan shook her head. "The main thing is to get back into life and keep living," she told them, walking to her car. The group was going to a nearby restaurant for lunch, but she was already feeling the strain of overexerting herself. It was time to go home. Balancing activity and rest was only one of the many new things cancer would dictate in Joan's life.

As Marilynn and Joan chatted, several choir members wished her luck with the treatment while offering to cook a meal or drive the boys somewhere.

"Thanks, we're fine," Joan said, getting into her station wagon. "My parents are here." Joan's assurance was genuine. There is no experience comparable to cancer so that one can be prepared. Later, there would be times when there would hardly be enough offers of help to offset the devastation of Joan's illness.

As the others left, Marilynn and Joan talked more about the chemotherapy and its possible serious side effects. "A little rougher than the picture you painted in choir," Marilynn said. "Your parents are still farming, aren't they? They'll have to go home to get the crops planted." Having raised two young children alone, Marilynn knew the struggle of getting everything done and determined to organize help for Joan when she needed it. But first, she would have to capture all the offers of help somewhere. After climbing into her own car, she pulled out a pencil and paper. Four people had offered help as they left that day. She wrote down their names and their offers. If Joan's chemo got tough, she would call them. Marilynn hoped she would not have to make those calls, but a nagging fear told her otherwise.

❖ *Five*

Jim forced himself to eat the breakfast his mother-in-law had prepared. It was not the food that bothered him, it was the steady buildup of emotions. Every day of the past few weeks had brought bad news, followed by good news, followed by worse news.

Having his in-laws, Maynard and Pauline Hutchinson, come stay while treatment got underway was a blessing in every way to Jim, to the whole family. He knew they wanted to be there helping. Maynard hauled the boys to their busy practice schedules and then stayed and watched. Pauline, used to cooking hearty meals for farm workers, provided plenty of tasty food for the four males in the house and she dug out special recipes for Joan to tempt her daughter's appetite.

"You've been here such a short time," began Joan's dad, his concern evident. He wanted the family to consider moving home to Iowa. "Who will help you?"

"We've already talked about it, Dad," Joan said, slipping into the chair between the men. She understood his worry. "Moving back to Iowa won't solve anything. It would uproot the boys right when they need things as normal as possible. Don't worry, we'll be fine. We can manage. We always have."

Jim quickly finished breakfast, spent a few minutes with Joan while she went over her plans for the day, kissed her good-bye, and then drove the forty-five minutes to his office. He wondered what the next bad news would be. Each day was getting worse. The more they found out, the more critical, more serious, more dismal the prognosis became. While preparing for his early morning run, he had prayed that they be allowed to catch their breath without anything else bad happening. It is one thing to try and think positively, but when one bad thing happens after another, a positive attitude can start seem out of reach.

As the general manager of a large window and door distributor, he usually arrived at work well before his staff to begin organizing the day. With the possibility of a harsh reaction to chemotherapy and more hospitalization for Joan, he planned to work even longer hours when he could to make up the hours he would miss on the Fridays when he was accompanying Joan to her treatment. These adjustments, while simple enough, added to the high degree of stress the Hendersons were already enduring.

When he opened his office door Jim was greeted by the stacks of paperwork that had piled on his desk during his absence. Before beginning to sort through it, he picked up the telephone and dialed their closest friends, Sue and Jim Brandl, who lived in Iowa. He needed to let off some steam.

Too often friends and even the spouse of an ill person do not realize the family has needs too during an extended or serious illness. The family's hearts are breaking as they stand by and watch their loved one struggle. They too may feel anger, guilt and fear, but can end up feeling isolated as everyone's energy is directed at the ill person. They may even assume since the illness has struck someone else they shouldn't feel bad.

"Our news keeps getting worse," Jim told Sue, explaining what the doctors had found. "I'm not even optimistic enough to pray for things to get better. But if we could just have one day where things don't get worse. We're handling what's happening, but I don't know where we'll get the strength to handle the next hurdle."

Sue listened quietly as Jim struggled to talk. There were moments of silence, but instead of speaking she gave him time to cry and begin again. "If anything else happens, I can't take it," he said in discouragement.

Sue's first thought was, Women don't die of breast cancer. She knew of many women who had mastectomies and continued to live. "So much progress and positive research has been done in this field," Sue said earnestly, but her words did not seem to give Jim much comfort.

Encouraged to do so by Jim, Sue called later when Joan was home alone. As usual, Joan immediately put her friend at ease. "Isn't this a bummer!" Joan said with a laugh, taking the edge off a difficult conversation. It gave Sue an opening to ask Joan about her fears but also to renew her hopes.

Sue felt she needed to hear what Joan was saying as much as Joan needed to say it, for she too was afraid of the unknown. She wanted to come into her friends' home, hold their hands, hug them tight, and help Joan with errands, but the distance did not give her those options. She hoped those who lived nearby were taking care of their daily needs while she looked for other ways to reach out with love to the family.

❖

This is what Jesus told his disciples. "I give you a new commandment, that you love one another. Just as I have loved you, you should also love one another. By this everyone will know that you are my disciples, if you have love for one another" (John 13:34-35). And so, when meeting the needs, it is to be done with a special attitude of love, described in 1 Corinthians. 13:4-8: "Love is patient; love is kind; love is not envious or boastful or arrogant or rude. It does not insist on its own way; it is not irritable or resentful; it does not rejoice in wrongdoing, but rejoices in the truth. It bears all things, believes all things, hopes all things, endures all things. Love never ends."

When caring within the church is based on God's kind of love, Christians become God's hands and glimpse the mighty power of the organized church—power that is within each Christian when God comes into their lives and that is unleashed when they allow God to work through them by actively sharing their God-given gifts and talents.

At first Sue and Jim called Joan and Jim weekly, then daily. The telephone became a lifeline where triumphs, along with pain, setbacks, and disappointments, were shared. It gave all of them an opportunity to talk out frustration and hurts and to keep connected—for Joan and Jim wanted to hear all about what was happening in the lives of their friends too.

Sue and Jim Brandl became the connection that relayed information to other mutual friends living in Iowa, saving the

Hendersons long distance telephone expense. The more they told others, the easier it became for the Brandls to talk about Joan's cancer and deal with it. It kept Joan constantly in their thoughts since people often came to them with questions and concern.

During one conversation Joan confided to Sue how she longed for the ordinary, everyday activities—to take the kids to school, to fix dinner, to feel halfway decent—not for the high points like buying a car or taking a vacation. She told Sue she was trying to survive for the sake of her husband and children. "Life is too precious not to try," she had said.

Because Sue could not always talk with Joan, she depended on letters to convey her thoughts and encouragement. She sent scripture, poetry, posters—all filled with hope and comfort. The letters also gave Sue an opportunity to send old snapshots to focus on the happy times they had shared. Even though miles apart, Sue's and Joan's friendship was never more fully alive.

Scripture seemed to take on new meaning for Sue. The strength of God's promises became real, and she began to make a notebook of verses that gave encouragement, assurance, and comfort. She sent the verses to Joan, each one written out on a 3-by-5 card so that Joan could keep them nearby. The Bible became Sue's comfort, a place to renew her strength for the journey ahead. She wrestled with anger against God. It seemed so unfair that her good and beautiful friend was suffering. She wondered why illness had struck the Hendersons and not her family. Even moments of guilt that she was healthy and Joan was not would invade her day.

Each day Sue prayed for Jim and Joan, the boys, and the doctors and nurses caring for Joan. She visualized a prayer covering like a clear plastic dome of protection to cover all she prayed for. As Jim and Joan mentioned the names of doctors or friends, Sue included them in her prayer covering. It was a constant reminder to her that one does not suffer alone. Each life touches those around it, and Jim and Joan were touching so many other lives through Joan's illness.

Sue could see the strength Joan's faith gave her, and she realized that she too could share Joan's courage and the spirit of her love. By speaking to groups, by writing a note of encouragement to someone who was hurting, by giving a smile, a squeeze, a hug—these were tributes to her friend that would continue on through her life and the lives of others.

In addition to praying for healing and health, Sue prayed for renewed strength, understanding, awareness, and peace. When she did not know what to pray for, she was silent, focusing on God, allowing the Holy Spirit to intercede for her.

Sue offered to come take care of Brian and Brent while Joan underwent chemotherapy, but Joan declined since Sue had teenage children who needed her at home. Instead, Joan invited the whole family for a week on the family houseboat. Their relationship had always been filled with humor, and cancer did not change that. Everyone kissed Joan's bald head each morning to make her hair grow back!

Along with the silliness, there was a chance to share deep feelings. As she rested on the couch and Sue fixed a meal, Joan began to cry. "I wish I could help," she said.

Sue knew it was important to let Joan cry and to allow her to express her inner feelings. How often Joan must have to hold her tears in because it was not the time nor the place, Sue reflected.

Once Joan told her friend, "I don't think I'm going to make it." Sue sensed it was not the time to disagree or to try and talk Joan out of her feelings. Joan had voiced a very scary, private thought, and it just needed to be left alone to settle.

Sue's husband Jim had played football with Jim Henderson at Central College and was Jim's closest friend. The two, along with a third good friend, Randy, had acquired the habit of reading through the Bible each year. They used a Bible that was divided into blocks of readings for each day. Occasionally they called each other to compare notes on especially meaningful passages.

Randy felt frustrated and handicapped by the distance. He too used the telephone to bridge the gap, supplementing calls with cards. Realizing both Jim and Joan had hurts, fears, and concerns, he alternated phone calls to both of them. They had always had a humorous relationship, and he did not hesitate to inject humor whenever he could.

Such conversations with his friends from the old days helped Jim release some of the anger and anxiety that built as Joan continued in treatment.

During a break in her tough chemotherapy and radiation regimen, Joan, Brian, and Brent had flown to Iowa for a week's visit with her parents, and Jim planned to drive out and pick them up. When he learned of Jim's plans, Jim Brandl re-routed his return home from a business trip to Florida. He flew into Nashville where he and Jim began their drive to Iowa. The trip was eleven hours of non-stop conversation about college, jobs, families, business, and life. As the men drove through Missouri and southern Iowa, the bright fall colors reminded them of their old college football days. The talk turned to old teammates.

"Seems like the older I get, the more I appreciate our football successes," Jim said, reminiscing. "It's a memory that can't be taken away."

For Jim, his friend's caring presence that day was like cool water on a parched throat. In the process of bringing Jim a memory of their shared past, they created a new memory of a day-long drive toward home, a day that was filled with laughter and warmth.

❖

As Joan and Jim plunged into treatment, they expected to handle homemaking chores and responsibilities like they had handled other challenges during twenty-one years of marriage. Both were more comfortable in the role of giver, not taker. Joan had grown up on the farm watching her mother, a petite, energetic homemaker, prepare meals for other families and her father spend extra hours in an injured or sick neighbor's field, getting a crop in. When Joan and Jim talked with their boys about sharing struggles, their examples always were of family and neighbors they had known for generations.

As they prepared to fight for Joan's life, they did not consider that neighbors whom they hardly knew would offer support. Most of the people they knew endured hour-long commutes to work and squeezed time in to taxi kids, coach ball, and participate in church and civic activities. No one had much free time for extra chores in their busy community. Besides, who would ask them to help? The Hendersons naturally assumed that they would have to handle the cancer alone.

After graduation and marriage, both Joan and Jim continued in coaching and teaching, and their ability to listen and think clearly drew students to them for practical advice and counseling. Methodical planners, they had waited five years to have their first child until they felt financially sound.

With this background, Joan and Jim had set two goals the day the cancer was diagnosed: first, to keep everything as normal as possible for Brian and Brent, and second, to fight the disease with everything they had. At the time neither one fully realized the magnitude of that commitment in terms of physical and emotional energy, time, and finances.

They braced themselves with the thought that if the chemotherapy was as exhausting as Diana and Cheryl had described, at least family life would remain routine for the first month with Joan's parents there. The cooking, cleaning, driving, and the family's spirit would be attended to through their presence.

"Mom and Dad, come sit at the kitchen table. We need to talk," Joan told her parents the evening before her first treatment. The kitchen table had been the meeting place when Joan was a child and continued to be so in her home. "I want to explain how we want to do this." When her parents were seated she continued, "I need you to stay at home and take care of the house and the boys to completely eliminate that concern for me. If you're here for the boys, I won't worry about them."

Maynard thoughtfully sipped his coffee. This was the way problems had always been worked out on the farm—whoever owned the problem was allowed to solve it in his or her own way with support from the family. "If that's the way you want it, okay," he said.

Pauline nodded her agreement too.

"Good. Tomorrow, I'm just going to say bye, and go."

Joan's mom smiled bravely. It was so hard to watch her daughter go through this. Joan had said she wanted no gloom and doom while they were there. They were trying, but keeping a smile was some of the hardest work Pauline had ever done.

❖

By Friday morning Joan was ready, almost anxious even, to get out of the house and meet Cheryl. Just as Diana had instructed, she ate plenty of carbohydrates and drank lots of liquid. Full of energy, she had taken a shower, put on a sweat suit and tennis shoes, and then fluffed her soft curls as she towel-dried her hair. She looked ready for tennis and, except for the way she gingerly held her left arm, she looked completely well. Her looking well would time and again contradict the knowledge that Joan was seriously sick.

As the time neared to meet Cheryl, Joan called Brian and Brent to come and sit with her on the couch. "I want to talk with you guys," she told them. There had been so much upset in their normally calm home, she needed to set the tone for what was coming. In keeping with the family agreement to be open and honest about all aspects of the cancer, Joan told them, "I can't tell you how sick I'm going to be tonight, but this is something I have to do to get well. We can look at the positive side and realize that being sick from the treatment is a part of getting better."

"What if something else goes wrong?" they wanted to know.

Joan looked from one worried face to the other. It hurt to see the fright in their eyes. She reached out and smoothed Brent's hair. "Then I'll tell you. I will never, ever not tell you what is going on with me," she promised. If they don't know, how can they trust, and how could she and Jim have conversations without fear of their overhearing? They had discussed those issues earlier at the hospital and agreed that trust could not be built on omissions and half truths. Brian and Brent might not like what they knew, but knowledge is strength no matter how old one is.

Both boys were glad for their parents' honesty. They wanted to be included, to know what was going on. They were scared, but at least they wanted to know what to be afraid of.

While Joan had promised to be honest, in truth, she had no way of knowing what effect the chemotherapy that morning would have on her. Her emotions ran the gamut, from fear and anxiety of the unknown to thankfulness that the treatment was available to her. As time went on, Joan would become more used to this roller coaster of emotional highs and lows.

"But I am feeling a little nervous, I think I need a hug."

"Oh, Mom," the boys chorused.

"A one-minute hug—come on you guys, everybody over here," she said. Jim, who had listened as Joan explained what was going to happen, joined them in a family-sized hug. The physical contact felt wonderful, and she could feel the tension draining away. When a minute was up she said, "That felt so good, I'll take one of those tonight. Before I go, I want you to know that I've talked with both your guidance counselors at school and explained what is going on with us. They'll let your teachers know. They both understand, and if you ever feel like you just need to get out of class and talk with someone, you can go to them or have them call us."

Joan and Jim initiated support from the school system by contacting the guidance counselors early, relieving the boys of the burden of sharing difficult information. "When we know what is going on, we can understand what's happening with the child and be there for them, and make allowances if necessary," Brian's junior high guidance counselor told Joan when she called. "It's good for their teachers to know so they can check in with a contact person if there seems to be a problem. Unless you know what's going on, it's hard to talk."

When her condition changed, Joan contacted the schools again to let them know what was going on. Later, when her condition worsened, she would drop in at school and take Brian out to lunch, just to break up the day and make contact.

Brent's teacher privately let him know that no single assignment was so important that it must be done and cause him to miss an opportunity to visit his mother. "We'll catch up on your work in the morning if there's a problem," she told him, then arranged for him to have less homework on the nights he planned to visit the hospital. "If you can't get to your homework, don't worry about it."

In fact, his only difficulty at school came from classmates who treated him extra nice. It was okay sometimes, but in truth Brent wanted to be treated like a normal kid.

From Diana's presentation four days earlier and by paging through the literature she had left, the Hendersons knew that chemotherapy reactions were a gray area that was always changing. As they drove out of their quiet neighborhood, both wondered what was going to happen during the next few hours.

❖

"There's Cheryl," Jim said, relieved. He pulled into First United Methodist's parking lot, dodging the overflow parking of high school students from across the street, one more reminder that life rushes on in the midst of problems. "Thank goodness she's on time!"

"Hi, guys," Cheryl said brightly, hopping from her car into their station wagon. Wearing a Christmas red corduroy jumpsuit, her waist-length hair falling in tangles down her back, Cheryl breathed life and energy as she banged the door shut. "Thanks for letting me come."

"Did we have any choice?" Jim asked, pretending to be solemn.

"No!" Cheryl countered the warm barb.

"Don't you have anything better to do on your day off?" Joan demanded.

"Nope, I'll do anything to get out of housework," Cheryl quipped. She knew she and Joan were going through a period of circling—when each tries to understand what the relationship will be as they begin to know the other beyond the boundaries of their usual friendship.

When the friendly bantering stopped for a moment, Joan admitted, "I'm feeling slightly nervous about all this."

"Joan, you're turning your well-being over to somebody else, trusting them with your life. It's normal to be nervous," Cheryl said, giving Joan a light pat on the shoulder.

"Where are we headed?" Jim asked as they neared the hospital parking lot. They were fortunate. An excellent cancer center, Nashville Memorial Hospital, was located just twenty minutes from their home.

"Around back," Cheryl answered. "I went through the check-in procedure yesterday, and everyone is super. I think you'll like them." Although Cheryl was a nurse, what she had done and continued to do throughout Joan's illness is something any support person could do. Previewing procedures helps to reduce anxiety.

Cheryl walked Joan and Jim through the cancer center, introducing them to the receptionists, and then took them back to meet the technicians and nurses. Both felt so vulnerable and off balance not knowing what kind of a reaction Joan would have to the medication, the procedures, or the personalities of the staff. Just having a third person with them was comforting.

Later, Jim told a woman whose husband was scheduled for chemotherapy, "If I had to do it again, and Cheryl wasn't available, I would ask a friend to drop by the cancer center the day before the first treatment to be walked through the check-in and treatment process. Having someone familiar with the process makes the ordeal easier. Not that they necessarily have special skills, but having someone there to help discuss a decision that needed to be made, or to wait with the patient while you go to get the car makes it so much easier."

The staff at Nashville Memorial was delighted with Joan. She was interested in what was going on around her. She wanted everything explained to her. And she was interested in everyone, treating nurses, technicians, and doctors like friends.

Even Joan's very formal oncologist, Dr. Miranda, a native of Chile, was to become her friend. When he continued to address her as Mrs. Henderson, she said, "If we are going to make this work, I need to feel you are a member of my team. I need for you to call me Joan."

"Oh, no, I couldn't possibly do that, Mrs. Henderson," he replied.

"We'll have to work on that together," she responded, but the ice had been broken.

That first consultation and treatment session was another sharp reminder of how serious Joan's condition was. As he discussed treatment, Dr. Miranda told them again, "We've got to get on top of this as fast as possible. The cancer is fast moving and aggressive."

As treatment progressed, staff members began to feel like a part of Joan's family and worked to make treatments easier for her. Even those not administering treatments to her stopped by her room to say hello and ask how things were going. "How's your daughter? What's happening in your class?" Joan asked right back, remembering a piece of information offered at their last meeting. It was not anything extraordinary that she did, it was just that she cared about the people helping her and let them know it.

Joan was neither helpless nor hopeless. She knew what her needs were and how to get them met. But some persons never get in touch with their needs and often those are the persons who do not ask many questions and do not take control of their situation. A patient's hopelessness and helplessness can affect the lives of their families. As patients become frustrated, they may abuse family members, drink, or use drugs. When these types of problems surface during an illness, hospital social workers can be consulted for help.

❖

"I hope nobody sees us because you look so drunk!" Cheryl teased Joan as the automatic doors to the cancer center swung open. The drugs had made her light-headed, so Jim had gone for the car while Cheryl and Joan waited inside. Joan was asleep by the time they pulled out of the clinic parking lot, waking only when Jim stopped to pick up a prescription at the pharmacy.

As soon as the car door slammed shut, Joan asked Cheryl, "How's Jim? How do you think he is doing?" Reassured by Cheryl that Jim was okay, she fell back asleep.

Cheryl thought, how like Joan to be concerned about another even when she's having difficulties. So many times during an illness she had heard friends express concern about the patient, forgetting that the parent or spouse was hurting too. Jim seemed so devoted to Joan, so strong and capable. It would be easy to overlook his needs.

❖ Six

A new kind of tension—wondering about the unknown and Joan's reaction to it—had filled the house. Her parents and children, alone all day with their own thoughts and fears, rushed to greet her, needing to see that she was okay.

"Hi, everybody," Joan called brightly from the hallway that night after chemotherapy. "I'll tell you everything, just give me a chance to get out of this jacket," she promised as the questions began to fly. She and Jim were beginning to understand the hospital system. Both the progression of the disease and its treatment took time. Tests and other people's emergencies delayed treatment. They had an education in the when, where, why, and how of cancer treatment that day, and that new knowledge had given them a sense of control. By sharing what had happened, she and Jim could draw the family in and help them understand what was going on with Joan instead of shutting them out.

Cheryl had picked up her car at the church, then followed Jim and Joan home. She asked Jim to get a piece of paper and followed him into the kitchen while Joan talked to her family. She arranged Joan's prescriptions on the counter, checked her watch and then with Jim's help, began to write down the actual time each pill was to be taken.

"Is this necessary?" Jim asked.

"Yes," Cheryl said simply. She knew that the staggered times of various medications could be confusing in the middle of the night or during a crisis.

Pauline had cooked a sumptuous dinner, putting nervous energy to good use, and the aroma of chicken baking in the oven reminded Cheryl she had another role to fulfill. She needed to get home and prepare a meal for her family. She left with the understanding that Jim would call her if they got into a tight spot. The doctor too had given them specific instructions, names, and telephone numbers in case of emergency.

Although Cheryl had offered to be a third set of ears and companion during chemotherapy, she had no way of knowing what that commitment would entail. Like Joan, she was a wife and mother in addition to her full-time nursing job and involvement as an active member of her church. To keep from over-extending herself or depriving her family, she would need to share her needs with others and gain their support.

She kept hearing a familiar voice in her head that echoed, "You cannot care for someone unless you take care of yourself." As a nurse, Cheryl had seen situations in which the caretakers wore themselves out. This only complicated matters.

She did begin to share almost immediately with her Sunday school class at Longhollow Baptist Church what was happening with Joan and Jim. Asking for prayers for them and herself was easy. As the class learned more about the Hendersons and the support group at First Methodist, they felt a need to meet Joan and Jim. Eventually Joan and Jim came to share with the class their faith and the meaning of stewardship.

As Joan's needs grew and Cheryl's role grew as well, Cheryl also could have benefited from a support group that provided occasional meals for her family or rides for her children. Simple information about her schedule with Joan revealed clues of types of help needed.

Joan was very sleepy from the nausea medication, but the baked chicken smelled so good she sat down with the family and delighted everyone with her hearty appetite following her first treatment. Talk centered on the chemotherapy. "The nurses wrapped my head with an ice pack to try to stop my hair from falling out," she said, trying to answer everyone's questions.

"Your mom did great," Jim said, winking at Joan. "She kept a cool head."

Brian groaned at his dad's pun, then asked, "How do they do the chemo?"

"Intravenously. It's not bad. And the nurses are really nice. One is going back to school."

"Sounds like you did a lot of visiting," Joan's dad said.

"They're people too, and they've got a tough job," Joan answered. "Besides, I'm not going to let people poke at me without knowing something about them." She had realized this was a team effort and wanted to know her team members.

Halfway through the meal everyone's questions about the therapy had been answered and talk turned to the boys' ball games, then Maynard told a story about the old days on the farm. The strain of the day evaporated around a shared meal.

Joan and Jim had been bombarded with so much information after surgery and at that first chemo session, and she felt so great following the treatment, they forgot about the time lapse between treatment and nausea. As she prepared to lie down in her bedroom, the nausea hit her. At 7:30 p.m., almost to the minute the oncologist said side effects might begin, Joan began to vomit, not a normal, flu-like vomiting, but violent, forceful vomiting that shocked her and Jim.

It was something like having a baby. Your mother and your friends may have told you all about it, but when it is your turn you finally understand what they were saying. Joan had read that she might vomit huge volumes forcefully, but still, she was losing control of her body, vomiting with such force it took her breath away, leaving her too weak to even wipe her face. Her only comfort was the knowledge that what she was experiencing was normal and expected. Still, the thought persisted, When does this end and when does the vomiting fall out of the "normal and expected" category.

"I don't want you to go through this. I don't want you to see me in this ugly state," Joan cried to Jim when she could catch her breath.

Jim wiped her face with a cool wash cloth and helped her back to bed. "Joan, I want to do this. Don't you see? It's something I can physically do to help you in the struggle. Let me be a part of the getting well process. I need to help."

She managed a weak smile. She knew it was hard for him to be around sick people, and she had worried about his reaction. Here was her answer.

He pulled a leather recliner into the bedroom and stationed himself by Joan's side all night, helping her to the bathroom every twenty minutes for the next thirteen hours, cleaning her up, then getting her back into bed only to repeat the process. He set the alarm clock to remind himself to give Joan her medicine at the times Cheryl had marked on the paper. He would never laugh at her again for being ultra-prepared. He had wavered on letting her come along. Now he was thankful she had offered.

At 8 a.m. the next morning he called Cheryl to let her know how the night had gone. It had been rough, rougher than he could have imagined. It was day one of treatment, with 210 days to go, and already he was exhausted.

He had made notes of Joan's reactions to medications throughout the night and relayed his concerns to Cheryl. Had Cheryl not been a nurse, he would have called his contact at the doctor's office.

"I can't believe she's so sick," Jim said finally, relieved to have someone to share information with.

"Nausea and other side effects have nothing to do with strength or coping skills, Jim. Just remember, she may be better or worse next month or just the same," Cheryl said.

She knew people often checked into the hospital for treatment because they cannot cope with vomiting like that. It can be a crisis for the patient and the spouse. But Joan wanted to stay at home with her family. This was a family crisis with the cancer affecting the whole family. She did not make them help, but she allowed them to see what the illness was doing to her.

Joan wrote in her diary: "What an awful thing to do to your kids, if you don't allow them to see you suffering and coping with the situation as it really is. If you have to have the macho image and put up a front . . . what a terrible thing for them to try to emulate."

But in public and around friends Joan downplayed her illness. Saturdays after chemotherapy she insisted on attending the boys' ball games; first basketball, then baseball. Surprisingly, the day after chemotherapy she felt well enough to go out. But by the second day after treatment, the horrible nausea and vomiting returned. Those who saw her at the ball games simply assumed she was doing great.

"Come sit with me," Cheryl called out at the first game Joan attended after chemotherapy. As they visited throughout the game, a half dozen people passing by asked, "Hey, Joan, how are you doing?"

"I'm fine," Joan said each time, sitting taller and smiling.

"Joan, why'd you say that? You're not fine," Cheryl demanded.

"What did you want me to say, I puked my guts out twenty-seven times?" Joan asked with honesty. Those who really wanted to know how she was doing would sit down and talk.

Even with all the anti-nausea drugs Joan took on treatment day, she continued to have eight to twelve hours of vomiting after the chemotherapy. Other side effects too began to take their toll. Over time, thirty percent of her heart function was lost, one foot and arm became numb, some days her eyes would not focus, and she began to suffer from vertigo.

It took a while to figure out her cycle of reactions to the drugs. One morning when Diane stopped by to visit, Joan complained, "I don't understand why I am so tired. I can't get anything done."

Even though the doctor had told Joan how she might feel, she needed to have the reasons explained again when those feelings became a reality.

"Remember, Joan, those drugs decrease the amount of oxygen in your body," Diane reminded her. "You must do less and rest more. If you'll keep a calendar of your good days and bad days after the chemo, you'll be able to plan for them the next cycle."

"All cycles might not be the same," Joan challenged.

"Then have an alternative plan."

Easy to say. Diane was healthy and energetic. She was able to sleep at night. She was not constantly worried about the future. But instead of leaving Joan with a piece of good advice, they sat down and Diane helped her design a plan. "First, let's make a list of the things you want to do."

Joan named a half dozen things, and Diane wrote them down.

"Now, what do you want to do most?" Diane continued. "Let's pick out the important stuff."

"Bells," Joan said.

"Okay, then how about giving up one of these other things?"

Under normal circumstances Joan would mentally list a day's activities, determine the priorities, get them all done, and have time to spare. Diane realized that day that the stress of the disease, the treatment itself, and the additional medication for side effects made things harder for Joan. But instead of taking over, she simply offered to help.

As treatment progressed, Joan kept track of good days and bad days. She learned that by the end of the three-week treatment cycle, she could look forward to five days of feeling decent, not pre-cancer stamina but less nausea and the return of some energy. The Thursday before her Friday chemo treatment left her feeling depressed, knowing the next day she would feel so bad again. She and Jim began to meet on that day for lunch to plan out the next couple of weeks. Joan kept a master calendar with the family's activities listed. Knowing what was coming up and how she would feel was an important planning tool to make the best of good days—days when they could schedule a trip to the houseboat, dinner at friends' homes, and other things to look forward to, instead of letting that precious time slip away.

❖

Brian and Brent's after-school routine kept Maynard busy with driving chores. He and Pauline were there to lift whatever burden they could from Joan and Jim and keep life normal for the boys. Their being there allowed the boys to have friends over, to get to dental appointments, get hair cuts, and go to ball games. They always had a ride to school if they missed the bus. Grandma was a great cook, and there was always something freshly baked after school to snack on.

Joan's parents were meeting many needs, but what of their needs? Their oldest daughter was fighting for her life. There was constant worry. They needed support too, and it came—from their friends and church in Iowa. Telephone calls with friends allowed the Hutchinsons to express some of the anxiety they felt and share what was happening with Joan and her family. Cards and letters reminded them almost daily that they were not alone, that others were thinking of them, praying for the family, showing that they cared. Certain friends wrote to them each week with news of home—helping them to feel less isolated. Two Iowa couples arranged their return trip from a vacation through Hendersonville to spend the night visiting.

Friendship Class members offered trips to the mall or an evening out, but both Pauline and Maynard refused. It was impossible for them to think of doing anything enjoyable when their daughter was so sick. Several at-home get-togethers with Joan's friends—coffee and short visits with a neighbor, a walk around the block with an opportunity to talk about the farm, or the good old days, or how to de-tassel corn, or Joan's condition—provided a small but needed release of tension. Talk turned to visitors' families and relationships grew as Joan's parents began to know local friends. Their confidence increased that Joan and Jim would have support when it was time for them to return to Iowa.

Planning became increasingly important after the first round of chemotherapy when Joan's father went home to get ready for spring planting. Joan's brother, Denny, had done much of the preparation, but it was a two-man operation and so Maynard needed to head home to Iowa.

Pauline stayed through the second cycle of Joan's chemotherapy. Joan's neighborhood friends had gotten together on an irregular basis before her cancer, and once Joan was through her first round of chemotherapy, they decided Joan and Pauline needed to get out of the house some. Pauline, who was calm and capable, seemed so grateful to be in Hendersonville and able to help her daughter. Yet she had been uprooted from her traditional support system, her friends and church. What could the support group here do?

They could simply listen. It was evident that just talking with others was helping her. It is sometimes very difficult to share deep thoughts with strangers. The group could begin to know her as a person, not just someone's mother who had come to help. They could, and did, create a climate where she felt comfortable in sharing by allowing her to know them. While friends were learning courage and seeing faith demonstrated through Joan's reaction to cancer, they were learning from Joan's family as well that this is the way a family cares for one another in a crisis. They were helping the way Joan and Jim needed them to help—without imposing their own agenda, their own rules, their own ways of doing things.

Finally, though, the time came for Pauline to return home too. An integral part of the farm, each day Pauline cooked and delivered lunch for her husband and son. Joan wanted her mother to be at home with her father, and after her second round of chemotherapy she insisted Pauline return home.

All during the time Maynard and Pauline had stayed in Hendersonville food was continually delivered to the house. Sometimes two or three people came by with a dinner or a desert on the same evening leading Maynard to remark, "I've lived my whole life in Iowa and probably don't know as many people as have brought in food!" The phone had practically rung off the hook, and the cards and notes had piled up.

Part of being able to leave their daughter was the confidence both parents had in Joan's support system. No one had done anything huge or grandiose. But many people had thought of something to do, then done it, sending the unmistakable message that Joan's supporters were doers.

After her mother left, Joan began to pick up her daily duties. In the beginning she tried to keep a normal pace but soon found it was impossible. Wearily she called Cheryl at Nashville Memorial. "I thought my heart would pound out of my chest when I went downstairs today," she said, lying down on the couch with a half-folded stack of laundry.

Anyone who had read Joan's literature would have been able to remind her that chemotherapy caused tremendous exhaustion. "Did you rest between chores? Remember, you must pace yourself," Cheryl said kindly.

It seemed to Joan that pacing was a difficult assignment when clothes needed to be washed, shirts needed to be ironed, and meals needed to be cooked. Barb had visited at the hospital and continued to check in on Joan. When she spied Joan struggling to iron, she told her, "Let me do that ironing."

Joan was ready to give it up, but it was hard to allow help, "No. You don't know how to iron."

"Watch me and see," Barb said, changing places with Joan.

Gratefully, Joan lay down on the couch but she could not resist one more challenge, "You know not to iron the emblems, you'll ruin them."

Barb laughed. It was Joan's way of keeping control—the give and take of bossiness.

Jim too tried to ease the way for Joan. One afternoon when she felt awful, he pulled out a stack of monthly bills and began writing the checks, a job Joan had always done. "Jim, I want to do that, don't take that away from me," she said.

He was surprised. He had thought that taking over some of her jobs would be helpful. But after thinking about it, he realized that relieving her of duties would put her into a helpless role, something Joan had never been. He was glad she had the courage to speak her mind. Other times when he cleaned up the kitchen on a good week, she gently reminded him, "I can do those things."

But there were things she could not do or should not do in order for her to get the rest she needed. Much of the food friends and church members had brought over was safely stored in the freezer by her mother for use when Joan took over. Jim and the boys could help when necessary.

❖

Some people began to reach out to the family in tangible ways. Others wracked their brains for a way to be useful, for within them was a need to show they cared—but how to do it? Wasn't there more to caring for a family in trouble than delivering a casserole? If so, what?

Why care? What do I have to offer? Who should I care for? These are three important questions when considering either individual caring or the creation of a support group. Consider that those without charisma, courage, or caring friends may be in more desperate need than those with attractive attributes. Or that many may have simply outlived or moved away from traditional support systems. Or, as Joan's situation developed, the family is self-sufficient and independent and simply assumes they will handle their cares and hurts alone.

But Jesus had a different plan, one that takes each "body" in the body of Christ, gives it a special gift, then expects that gift to be used to benefit the other bodies.

Each Christian has a spiritual gift, given at the point of salvation when Christ is received into a person's life, but it is up to each individual to discover their gift. How? By exploring and investigating the various gifts, trying them out, asking others who are informed for insight, and listening to their own sense of God's direction. Affirmation of your gift may be a peace you gain about it, an ease you have using it, or a success God brings from your exercising it.

For whom should we care? For the Friendship Class caring for Joan, a person who just had surgery was an obvious choice. We can remember times in our own lives when a supportive or caring presence would have been welcome: a move to a new city or church, illness or injury in the family, marital separation or divorce, jail term, death of a relative or friend, loss of a job, problems with children.

Haven't we all ignored our own instincts and found out later they were correct? Do we need to see someone go under for the third time before we jump in and offer a hand? Do we avoid possibly embarrassing others by ignoring their needs or making ourselves uncomfortable by their possible refusal of our help? Is not embarrassment better than a need not met? Could the discomfort be recognized and smoothed over by stating our own need to act instead of standing idly by?

❖

The weeks immediately following Joan's diagnosis had zipped by in a blur of activity; the biopsy, mastectomy, consultation, treatment startup plus physical healing were all time-consuming, exhausting, and painful. The Hendersons did not think about getting help organized. With Joan's mom back in Iowa, several people offered to cook a meal, and Joan agreed. She thought if a meal was provided the day of chemotherapy and maybe the next day their special needs would be taken care of. She would cook the rest of the time. Joan was an excellent cook, but once chemotherapy began the smell of cooking made her extremely nauseous, and the anti-nausea medicine put her in a light-headed stupor.

While the first showing of support calmed worries about who might help, a structured support group could provide stability. In large churches, members may assume someone else is helping; in small churches, that no one else can help. Tasks that are defined and assigned prevent both too much and too little help.

The Friendship Class had several characteristics that made organizing help for the Hendersons successful. The class had formed two years before Joan's diagnosis and was filled with people who were casual friends. Many members of the class were newcomers to Hendersonville, were about the same age as Joan and Jim, had children the same age, and shared similar lifestyles. They had only to imagine themselves in the same situation to realize the help needed.

Joan's cancer diagnosis had shocked and saddened class members. As observers, members experienced a variety of emotions—grief, fear, anger, hope, despair—that could have paralyzed the class into a state of inactivity. Many class members cared, they wanted to do something, but they did not know what to do, or what others were doing, or what was left to do.

Joan and Jim, while asking for prayers at the onset of the cancer diagnosis, were quick to let everyone know they were facing the crisis as a family. Both were intelligent, organized, energetic, and in good financial condition. All outward appearances suggested they could handle cancer better than most. For the class to suggest that they needed help seemed an intrusion, almost an insult—as if they could not handle it on their own. But Joan wrote a letter to the church to be read to several Sunday school classes they had attended. It gave everyone new insights. Cancer meant different things to different people. Until then it was unclear to most people exactly what Joan's prognosis was.

I want so much to talk or write to each one of you personally, but to date my "active times" have been very brief—thus a form letter.

Just two weeks ago I had surgery that told us we are dealing with an advanced stage of rapidly-moving cancer. The odds and the prognosis are the bad news. The good news is that my body gave a warning it needed HELP! The doctors said I have a tricky form of cancer; it usually gives no warning and consumes a person. This is a clear sign that God has plans for me. My bone and liver scans were clear of cancer which is great news. I have a strong body to fight these bad guys. With those two scans clear, a brain scan was not ordered at this time. I think that was a real blessing too. There is still no proof that my brain is small and thick, only speculation.

Because of the advanced stage of the cancer, we started chemotherapy just four days after leaving the hospital. I say "we" because this is a family effort. It went well. Not exactly a picnic, but with a sense of humor we did great. Each time I'm sick, Jim reminds me the chemicals are working. Brent thinks of them as little "Pac Men" going through my body destroying the sick cells. Not bad thinking for an eight-year-old.

Because the chemicals are so strong, I'll have intravenous treatments every three weeks for a year. Some radiation will be sandwiched into that schedule. Actually there was a sense of comfort when the oncologist said the treatments would be for one year. At least he thinks I'll be around for a year. I plan on surprising them all.

The last two weeks have been challenging and I know the weeks ahead will have lots of little "kinks." But God loves me so much and has surrounded us with such a calm that I hold tight to his promise, "All things work for the good to them that love God." I have felt your prayers and can't tell you how much your love and thoughtfulness have meant to us during this difficult time.

Love,
Joan

Because she asked for prayers and accepted the first meals that were provided after surgery she gave others "permission" to offer help. A vital part of the equation was information about the disease and its treatment. Access to information about the changing effects of Joan's cancer treatment was available through Diana, the oncology nurse. Joan often acted and looked healthier than she was. Although she alluded to a rough time in chemotherapy, her upbeat attitude made it seem less difficult than it actually was. Just a couple of weeks after her first chemotherapy treatment, Joan was at a class work project dishing up hot soup from the back of her station wagon and trading jokes with workers. Without Diana's insight the class simply might have missed many opportunities to help.

❖ *Seven*

"The class needs to know the real story," Diana told the Friendship Class members one Sunday. "There are too many expressions of false hope in spite of all that we see. It places an expectation on Joan that she has to get well."

Diana was right. When class members heard good news about Joan, even if it was not factual, they fed it back to Joan, putting pressure on her to get well. Helpful support came when people became realistic. Once they began to know what was going on with Joan, people began setting up a realistic environment that was comforting.

Joan and Jim found it helpful to set up definite lines of communication that were open but narrow. One classmate was responsible for checking with them for information about Joan's condition and reporting back to the class. People sometimes share information with their own slant, and limiting the amount of shared observations decreased misinformation.

"The support system worked out as if there was this grand scheme of how we should work it out," Joan wrote in her diary. "But actually it fell together."

The basis of the support group originated with a handful of people who listened to Joan and Jim, asked questions, received good information, saw possibilities, asked permission to act, organized a system that excluded no one, implemented the plan, and made changes when necessary. Group interaction and discussion allowed the group to benefit from the experiences and ideas of others. The group's energy, enthusiasm, experience, and empathy created a gift of love.

Groups organizing support for ill persons will find it helpful to invite an expert into the organization to give the human side of the disease. The person could be a nurse, a doctor, or a social worker with expertise in the specific illness. The patient will generally feel relief that people understand the disease and its treatment. A current resource center for health issues within the church library would be helpful and could be kept updated by donations of literature by patients and families no longer needing it.

Jim agreed that having Diana keep the class updated on Joan's treatments helped both of them. "It was comforting to know the Sunday school class had accurate information. Diana was a link, a medical person who shared some of our same beliefs within the church, who could share information about Joan's cancer with the class. Joan wanted them to understand her physical condition."

Mary MacArthur, Joan's hospital social worker, explains the importance of accurate information: "People make value judgments on the state of other people's needs. We say, 'They could have done that themselves.' We have a Protestant work ethic; people should do pretty much what they can do and what they can't do, we're there to chip in for them. But sometimes looks can be deceiving. Joan would appear to be better than she was and, with Jim going to work and the boys to school, things appeared more normal than they were. That is why it is so important to know the nature of the illness when you are organizing support for people."

When Joan began treatment, class members and friends wondered what they could do to help. A doctor had said living the ten months until Christmas would be a miracle. The family's decision to fight the cancer head on and their wish to keep life as normal as possible allowed friends an opportunity to share in the fight by taking some of the jobs Joan and Jim wished to give up. By shouldering even a small amount of the burden, church members helped to save Joan's energy for treatments or for spending time with her family. "Love one another as I have loved you," Jesus said (John 15:12). The church needed to love the Henderson family by being allowed to help them. It was a new concept for many people. Traditionally giving through the church had been to aid missions or for the poor, not for one of their own.

It was important for people to say to Joan and Jim, "We're sorry about your situation, we want to be in this with you, we want you to count on us." But it was awkward too, because many who wanted to help did not know them well.

❖

Marilynn and Cheryl R., both members of the bell choir and the Friendship Class, knew from conversations with Joan that some chemotherapy patients walk out after treatment and feel pretty good, whereas others remain bedridden. By Joan's sheer strength of will it seemed she might get through the therapy okay. But after observing Joan's reaction to just two cycles of chemotherapy, Marilynn and Cheryl knew Joan was not one of the lucky ones. On Marilynn's follow up telephone call to check on her friend, Joan described to Marilynn how nauseated the smell of food made her.

Others too were aware that providing meals on a regular basis would help Joan, and a few of those persons met to discuss the best way to organize a way to offer the meals that would make it easier for the Hendersons to say yes. Cheryl had been a member of the Friendship Class for a year when Joan was diagnosed with cancer. A stroke she had suffered while her daughter was a toddler made her aware of the needs of ill persons. Within her was a need help someone else, and as an organized person she could make sure plans became a reality.

Marilynn considered taking a monthly calendar to bell practice so that members could sign up for a day to cook for Joan; but first she discussed it with Cheryl and Joan's good friend Cathy. They agreed to talk it over with Joan and Jim.

Cathy wanted to help Joan because she cared about her, not because it was expected. An organized person who packed many activities into her day, Cathy and her husband Don shared similar values with Joan and Jim. Cathy respected Joan and saw her as a person in control of her life. She knew Joan did not have an "Oh, you poor thing" disposition and would not receive help if it was offered in that manner.

The women realized that in order to be successful, the offered help would have to be individualized for the Henderson family and would require cooperation among a number of different people and groups. Also, it would require commitment on the part of those participating, especially the chairperson who would act as a buffer between the cooks and the Hendersons. The chairperson would not necessarily have to be a close friend, just someone who was committed and organized.

Cheryl and Cathy went to the Henderson home to share their thoughts. "There are a lot of people who want to help, that want to get involved," Cathy said explaining their plan. "You'd be doing them a favor to allow them to cook."

Joan arched her eyebrow. "Now why would some stranger want to spend their evenings cooking for me?" she asked with a laugh.

"Not strangers, Joan, people at church, around the neighborhood, they're all feeling very helpless," Cheryl explained.

Joan and Cathy had talked about help for a long time. "Now," Cathy reasoned, "your friends want you to spend your energy getting well."

Jim nodded his agreement with what Cheryl and Cathy were saying. The way they explained it made him feel he was doing something good for others by accepting their help. They had put a new twist on the old adage—"It is more blessed to give than to receive"—by showing him that others could not receive the good feelings, the blessings that come with being a giver if he would not be a receiver.

Once the offer of food was accepted, the chairperson made a list of specific foods the family liked and disliked, food allergies, special menus, dinner times, and other details, putting all the information on a food calendar. While in treatment some patients may need to eat at a specific time, or avoid certain foods, or eat certain types of food such as bland foods due to nausea. Preparing suitable foods prevents the family from cooking just for the sick person. Cooking favorite soups or special foods for the patient may be a task several cooks take on while others prepare meals for the rest of the family.

Marilynn's food calendar, passed through both choirs and many Sunday school classes, was a way to get offers organized on paper. Persons put their name on the calendar and they put what food they planned to provide in order to avoid delivering meat loaf three nights in a row and other mix-ups.

Cheryl agreed to become responsible for keeping the calendar. Her job was to determine what meals Joan and Jim needed, then do the legwork to provide them. From the original calendars passed through the church, Cheryl had the names and telephone numbers of those who had been willing to cook. She announced in several Sunday school classes the organization for cooking meals and asked to be contacted if anyone else wanted to be added to the list of cooks. Members of several clubs Joan belonged to were also informed of the plan and additional names were added to the list.

When Cheryl had the designated dates filled for a month, she made a copy of the calendar with the cooks' names, menus, telephone numbers, and each day's menu filled in for Joan. That way Joan had control over the meal. If she needed to cancel at the last minute or change a delivery time, she could do so.

For Jim and Joan, the knowledge that thirty different persons were cooking during a month made the meals easier to accept. They felt less like they were imposing. Jim said, "We didn't realize how many people actually had this great need to help, even those who we didn't know."

For Jim, having just two friends come to their home to talk about their needs was comfortable. And the offer of a chairperson to organize the meals, thus acting as a buffer between his family and the many helpers, made it more appealing as well. "If it had been left up to us, some of those things would have never happened because we simply did not have the time to deal with it, arranging the meals, finding out what time they are going to arrive. Plus, we simply wouldn't have asked. Emotionally too, we couldn't take the risk of rejection. If it had been up to me to request a meal of someone and they had said, 'Gosh, I can't tonight,' I would have been crushed. The last thing we wanted to be was a burden!"

One night Jim returned home from the hospital after Joan had been admitted for a few days. There was a list of five persons who wanted to prepare meals but had not contacted the food chairperson. "I couldn't call them. I had gotten home late, and I figured they would understand why I had not called. It was an easy out. I was really tired at that point, really worn out emotionally. To communicate with each person about a meal, I'd also have to go through what was happening with Joan and I really struggled with that. They'd say, 'How are you feeling?' or 'How are the boys doing?' Joan was not doing well, work was tough, I was concerned about the kids, everything was building up, and I was hitting rock bottom. So, I'd either have to lie and say, "We're doing great," or I would have to emotionally go through it all again. So if I had to look forward to making five of those kinds of phone calls, you can see it wasn't worth the return. It was easier to think about running out for hamburgers or a pizza."

The food calendar and the chairperson to manage it was also perfect for church members. By it's very nature, it limited and defined what was expected. Sometimes offering help can be as uncomfortable as accepting it. What do you say to the family of someone diagnosed with cancer? The person offering to cook may feel he or she will call at the wrong time, break down and cry, say the wrong thing, or be refused. Working through a chairperson made it easier for those doing the giving.

For those who wanted to provide a meal but did not have time to cook, there were other options. Joyce, another class member, was starting a business, and with two kids and a busy schedule, had little time to cook. But she felt a sincere need to help. Her contribution was having pizza delivered. "It was easy to do. I just went by and told them what time to send the pizza, paid for it, and left a tip for the driver."

The changes in menu were particularly enjoyed by Brent and Brian. Brian explains: "When the family says it doesn't matter what food you send, it does!" For families with children, he suggests fewer casseroles, plain fruit, cleaned vegetables, brownies, cookies, soft drinks, chili, pizza, and food coupons for fast food restaurants, plus offering to cook a favorite family recipe.

"It seemed neat, people doing things to help," says Brian. The Hendersons were discovering that a sense of community—people entering into other peoples lives to help—was not something from the old days on the farm or a relic from the past. It was here too, a visual show of love.

The food calendar was successful because it matched strengths with tasks. Those who wanted to cook signed up, informing the chairperson how often they wanted to be called. And delivering the meals was keeping people in touch with the family who normally would have rarely seen them.

With feedback from the family, cooks learned that six rolls are adequate while twenty-six rolls are excessive. They learned that when food is brought in nightly, leftovers can create problems because they either have to be stored or thrown away. The family did not want elaborate meals; in fact, sometimes just macaroni or hot dogs was welcome. Some cooks simply doubled what they were cooking at home for their family.

One time Jim counted twenty-seven dishes and pans left by friends at the house. All dishes should be marked by the cook. Many types of containers look the same. Disposable containers that can be tossed instead of washed are preferable.

When delivering food it is wise to keep the visit short unless a family member needs to talk. In Joan's case, at certain times she was extremely susceptible to germs and visits were dangerous.

Joan and Jim's appreciation of the meal, a simple thank you, and the knowledge that a burden had been lifted were thanks enough. "I felt helpless," said one friend. "It helped me to at least feel I was doing something, although taking cookies didn't change anything."

When meals were not needed, other foodstuffs were appropriate—snack foods for the boys, special treats, soft drinks, a jar of popcorn—items taken for granted until there is a money crunch.

Jim remembers that the plates of cookies and cakes that were dropped off at the Hendersons' by church members allowed Joan to maintain a special routine with a little help.

"There were certain times each day that Joan wanted everything to be perfect. One of those times was after school. That stemmed from when she was a kid on the farm, and her mom would have something freshly baked coming out of the oven. Joan always wanted to be there when Brian and Brent came home from school. She sat on the front porch, waiting for each child, then talked over the school day at the kitchen table while eating a special snack. With chemotherapy, she was much too sick and weak to mother the kids the first week. By the second week, she would start back to the old routine, setting her alarm clock to wake up from a nap at the time the boys were coming home from school, serving the sweets that friends had brought."

❖

Extending help to the family turned into a positive experience for everyone. "In Joan's case, many people learned the joy of giving," recalls Brother Ben. "Joan and Jim's gracious acceptance of the help of others made the giving of that help a blessing. The way a gift is received often dictates the fun of giving the gift or the meaning of the gift to the giver. Each gift has a meaning for the giver as well as the recipient."

That was true for one friend who said, "Because of my relationship with Joan, I am happier, more laid back than I used to be. I'm able to focus on things that really matter. Part of that definition comes from Joan, the importance of personal relationships."

Joan's upbeat attitude and her belief in God changed one member of the class who had been diagnosed with multiple sclerosis. An artist, Suzie had lost half of her vision and was furious with God. "What had I ever done to deserve this?" she wondered. She fell into a deep depression. "I think it would have taken me a lot longer to get with it if it hadn't been for Joan. I did not know her well at all but I went to see her in the hospital and when she was at home. I think my visits did more for me than for her. It's a very scary feeling to be out of control and to know there was nothing I could do.

"I began to relate to her situation; both of us had something that was not going to go away. Since then I have figured out a lot of things. It didn't have to do with God, it had to do with disease. I have come to the conclusion that God can help you with diseases. Now, I think I am a better person for having MS. Life is what you make it whether you have cancer or MS or whatever."

Cheryl R. was receiving too, even as she gave. "Through Joan, I also learned a lot that translated to other situations. She showed us that if we just hold tight to our faith, our families and our friends, we'll make it through, or at least we'll be better off. The resolution to our trials may not be what we want it to be, but if we have faith, we'll be able to understand and handle the answer we get from God."

This is the way that one classmate described becoming involved. "It's like the promotion they run for Special Olympics when all the kids are racing for the finish line, and one runner stumbles and falls. The crowd jumps to its feet with a gasp, but nobody moves. For a moment, the event turns ugly as the fallen runner looks around in bewilderment. Then one of the racers turns back, forgetting all about the race, and helps the runner to her feet. A warm glow comes over the whole event. The outcome of that race is not changed, but no one can take away the glow. Our Friendship Class was committed to providing as much of that warm glow as possible."

But Joan still had difficulty in letting others help take care of her home and sons and husband. She did not want to impose on people by allowing them to do things for her, things that she could not repay. In time, Mary MacArthur helped Joan to see that allowing help was the most practical application of what faith is all about.

"We're here to support each other and to be Christlike to each other," Mary said. "You feel good when you do things for other people, why won't you let others have a good feeling by helping you? When you talk about repayment, what does it mean? When the giving is done, the giver feels repaid already!"

She turned the situation around. "Joan, if you did this for somebody, would you expect repayment? What would you want as repayment?"

"I wouldn't want repayment," Joan admitted.

As Joan learned to be more comfortable receiving help that she could not repay, she explained her feelings to Patsy, a Friendship Class member and psychologist who was gathering reference material on helping behaviors for nursing students. "It doesn't really matter what the gesture is. It's just that somebody takes the time to call or write the note or bake the cookies. It's just that people take the time to say, 'I'm here.' They don't have to say anything really. They don't have to say, 'It's really crummy that you have cancer, and I'm sorry this is happening.' They don't have to have any profound words of wisdom, because there aren't any. They just say, 'I'm here.' Or they say, 'I love you, I'll help you.'

"They give the common sense things. If we need groceries, someone goes and gets the groceries. It was hard for me to accept all that. It's easier to be a doer for somebody else than a receiver.

"Then, you put it into perspective. That's the whole scheme of loving and the backbone of Christianity—to love thy neighbor as thyself and I had no right to deny them that feeling of helping us if that was important to them. It was definitely important to me. I just had to overcome my feelings of being on the receiving end instead of on the giving end.

"I don't have much trouble with it anymore because I couldn't do it without them. But it did take me a while because it meant giving up my can-do image."

While Joan came to depend on help from others, friends could not get through the week without doing something tangible for the family. Someone mowing the yard meant that Jim had an extra two hours to do something more important, someone providing homemade chicken soup meant that Joan, who was becoming thin and frail, might be tempted to eat.

A friend did not realize until much later that the weekly horseback riding lessons she arranged for the boys benefited the entire family. When she was well enough to go, Joan enjoyed watching the boys have fun. At other times, it meant she simply rested more easily knowing that the boys were active; that Jim was released from responsibility for an hour—time enough to eat a bowl of ice cream or watch television—and that the boys' focus was turned to something new and challenging.

❖

While others were working to provide ways to help, Joan was determined to keep some things the same at home. Jim's birthday was coming up, and she planned to celebrate it the way they always had. Birthdays were special occasions with her, and cancer was not going to rob the family of those joys. She had wrapped presents and cooked a huge meal. When everyone was finished eating and the presents unwrapped, she sent Jim and the boys out to play football while she watched out the kitchen window and loaded the dishwasher. As she cleared away dishes from the table, sheer exhaustion suddenly overwhelmed her and she collapsed sobbing at the table.

"What's wrong, Mom?" Brent had come to see what was taking her so long.

She wiped the tears away, angry that she had cried in front of Brent, that she was crying on Jim's birthday. Later that night the tears came again as Jim held her. "I don't want to die and leave the kids," she cried.

Jim realized Joan was more exhausted than she let on, and he worried about going to work and leaving her home alone. He called Cathy and worked out a plan to assure that Joan was okay during the day while he was gone. They planned for church members and neighbors to spend the day at the Henderson home "babysitting" Joan. Their intentions were good, but they made one mistake, they did not consult Joan.

"You two have my life all planned out," she said, turning down the plan.

"We quickly learned to ask Joan how she wanted something handled," Cathy said. "It was important for Joan to call the shots. You take away a person's self-respect and self-esteem by taking over. She was still in control, it was her life. You can't help by running over someone.

"Our job was to be an enabler—to enable her to be as whole a person as she could be by providing those parts of functions she couldn't perform at the time, then letting them come back to her as she was able to take them on again."

Instead of tossing out the entire plan, they asked, "Is there any part of this that works?" Joan felt that she did not need someone with her all the time. She chose instead to allow someone to drop by her house for a few minutes after the boys left for school. As a conscientious mother, she did not want to take other mothers away from their children before school. Since Jim's office was forty-five minutes away, Joan also consented for one person to commit to be

To Be the Hands of God

home each day and kept that person's telephone number handy, just in case.

"It's important that we still require roles of people with cancer rather than put them in a sick role. And it's extremely important to ask how the sick person wants things done. It shows that you see them as in control and having the best information on their situation instead of, I know what's best for you," Mary MacArthur says.

Joan told Patsy's nurses, "Difficult is not a big enough word for having to open up and allow others to help. Then Brother Ben told us that we are put on this earth to support and love everybody, that's God's whole plan. And if we are Christians, which we profess to be, that part of the process is to allow people to get fulfillment by helping you. But it's like all the rest of this, it hasn't been easy."

Mary MacArthur says, "You saw someone who really made a decision that was a conflict. She had a bigger part of her that said, 'I need to accept this help and open up to it, because it's something that will help everybody.'

"Joan embraced that wonderful permission you can get when all of a sudden there is a limitation imposed on your life. That permission was, 'Well, I can either go through this by myself and be that prideful person that wants to be a little bit in the background or I can share this stage of my life with those around me and be more fully alive.' And that is what it is about when you connect with other people. She invited other people into those personal things that were going on. What it comes down to in the long run is, what is it really going to profit me to go through this by myself?

"Joan is what I would call a well-developed person. She lost some of her functions and some of her roles. She couldn't teach a college class, but she could still teach individuals and share experiences. She might not always be able to be the wife and mother she wanted to be, but there were still parts of that. She was still a mother, people still needed her, that was very, very important. It may be important that we still require roles of people with cancer, rather than put them in a "sick" role, i.e. 'I still need you as my wife,' translates to, 'I still see you as a competent person.'"

Jim agreed, "Joan had always been the counselor in our family. When I was down, she put things into perspective after allowing me or the kids to say all the things we were feeling. Cancer never took that role away from her."

Naturally the support group made some mistakes along the way and learned some things too. A list of birthdays and other special occasions would have provided opportunities to help the family celebrate with a special meal. The church is the home of some of the greatest cooks in the world, witness the dessert table at any church gathering. With special dates on a food calendar, these dessert makers would have had an outlet for their talents by baking birthday or anniversary cakes for the family. A regular group of drivers would have made it easier for family members, especially children, to get to the hospital to see the patient. More planned activities for the children would have allowed Jim more time to relax and given Joan the knowledge the boys were having some fun. Coupons for pizza or for dinner at a local restaurant would have meant an opportunity for the family to get out and do something different. An invitation to dinner may have been just what the family needed to forget about their worries for a few hours.

The key to helping is reaching out with sensitivity. If our efforts are brushed off at first, we cannot take it personally. If the patient is in treatment, and if we feel help is truly needed or appropriate and we are not getting anywhere with our offers, we can call the hospital and ask for a social worker's advice. Or ask our minister to make contact or help us get started.

Being supportive does not mean taking over or telling the family or the patient what is to be done or when. Being supportive is finding those areas where the family wants help, and then doing them the way the family wants them done.

❖

The church support plan was written throughout Joan's illness, mistakes and all, until it evolved into a coordinated program that took into account the needs at each stage of Joan's treatment and physical condition. What was missed at first due to inexperience or ignorance was made up for with gusto and commitment. The development of the plan was a learning experience for everyone. The Hendersons and the support group learned together as they became a team, each meeting the other's needs. The plan came to work so well that eighteen months into her illness, Joan told a Sunday school class, "The support group and friends took away all those mundane hassles of everyday living. It was a tremendous burden taken from us. We needed to concentrate on surviving as a family."

While Joan fought the cancer, people interacting with her were seeing her celebrate life as something that was not going to end with death. It was not so much what she said, but rather an attitude about life that was a powerful witness to the whole church.

"The church through the years had held before Joan the truth of continuing life," Brother Ben said. "Jesus said he came to bring abundant life, and Joan believed that. Joan knew that God loved her. Because she knew that, she could face both life and death. That knowledge was a foundation for her life. It was a strength for her in facing death and should be for all of us. The congregation saw in Joan an example of God's love at work in a person. And that love was contagious and easily caught if you were around her. I think she taught us how to live and how to die."

And, as the Hendersons accepted acts of caring, the community grew in its love for the family. As understanding of the dynamics of Joan's illness and the far-reaching effects of help grew, so did the desire and willingness of others to become a part of their struggle. In subtle ways, Joan's illness, and her family's reaction to it, was causing people to reexamine the way they thought about disease, about God's connection to it, about life, and about relationships.

❖ Eight

From November to January, Joan was fairly strong and active. A tight nucleus of support came from the Friendship Class. But the quantity and quality of response from others, both individuals who responded on their own and members of other Sunday school classes who worked with and through the Friendship Class, was tremendously uplifting, giving the family a feeling of strength.

The church choir signed up for meals on Marilynn's food calendar and then devised their own visiting calendar. They respected the Hendersons' need for family time and Joan's need for rest, and by scheduling visits they hoped to maintain a balance between too many visits and too few.

At the very beginning of Joan's cancer treatment, an individual church member unwittingly helped Jim when they met at a local ice cream parlor. Dave and his wife had talked about Jim's reaction to Joan's cancer and how well he seemed to be handling the additional responsibilities. But they also had talked about how hard it must be to be the spouse of someone who had cancer. "How are you?" Dave asked Jim as they waited for their ice cream.

Jim responded, "Joan's doing really well with her treatments." Jim was so focused on Joan, he had been asked so many times how Joan and the boys were that he naturally responded to Dave's question with an answer about Joan.

"No, how are *you*? I'm really wondering, how is Jim? I want to know about you." Dave did not know it, but it was the first time someone had asked Jim how Jim was doing. Jim mumbled something about how he was hanging in there as he paid for the ice cream. Dave suggested they get together for lunch. In a few days, he made a phone call to Jim to set a time. The show of concern validated the fact that Jim was suffering too and needed someone to show interest in him.

Don also recognized Jim's need and began calling him soon after Joan's diagnosis to meet for lunch on a weekly basis. He knew from his pastoral training and work that whoever is ill gets most of the attention. Don was concerned about Jim and how he was faring. He would ask Jim, "How are you today?" Don knew that Jim could more easily talk about how Joan was doing than about his own feelings.

Don also felt that most people can solve their own problems if allowed to talk. He was intentional in keeping their lunch dates and out of that grew a very close friendship.

In addition to the help she was receiving from others, Joan turned to literature. She had always felt close to God, but now she started each morning with *Guideposts* stories and a daily inspirational reading.

She and Jim also gave to others. When they were approached by the church to give a brief talk, Joan accepted—then got cold feet and Jim spoke.

When Patsy, a class member and psychologist, asked for help with a special project, Joan agreed enthusiastically. Patsy wanted Joan's thoughts on caring and wanted to tape record an interview with Joan to use later to educate and sensitize her nursing students.

"There are always good things," Joan said. "But that doesn't mean you don't have to look a little deeper for them or try to see something in a different light. Our church and our neighbors—their support group has just been phenomenal. When we have been down, people have literally picked us up."

She went on. "It's something that I can hardly comprehend, let alone explain. It's that unconditional love which the Christian faith is all about. How people deal with cancer or illness without that kind of support, without that kind of personal faith, I don't know. It would be awful, you would feel so alone. Somebody once said to me, 'Don't you feel alone?' No, because people have always been there who have said, 'We are here, we will help you.' Maybe that is why I don't have a sense of panic about what we have been through, or what we are facing now, or the death issue."

Just as supporters helped Joan and Jim over the rough times, so too did they plan celebrations for them. Chemotherapy had been rough. At one point, Joan wrote, "Forcing myself to go back was a real experience. Jim kids me about leaving heel marks on the front walkway while he pushes me out to the car on treatment days. But if you get hit by a truck, you don't usually go stand in front of another one!"

The end of chemotherapy was a major milestone for the Hendersons, and neighbors recognized a celebration was in order. They had said all along, "When this is over, we're going to have a party." Just looking forward to the party brought pleasure. A dozen families greeted the Hendersons at a pot-luck pool party with congratulations and plenty of teasing. Even a sudden thunderstorm that knocked out all the power for most of the evening could not dampen everyone's spirits. Jim remembered another social event when Joan went back into the kitchen and found people crying. But this was different. This was the group that was most like her, the group that teased her and Jim unmercifully, the group that always stood by them.

"Don't forget, this doesn't end," Joan told the crowd as the desserts were brought out.

The next week Joan began six weeks of maximum radiation. Each day she prayed, "Lord, get me through this." And He did.

But again, Joan looked better than she actually was, and now she insisted on driving herself to treatment, part of her wanting to be independent and in control. "If I need help, I'll call," she promised worried friends. She was handling it the way she wanted.

When the radiation treatments ended, Joan and Jim and the boys were ready for a desperately needed vacation. They decided to go to Disney World. Treatment was over, doctors told Joan she had done beautifully, leading them to shorten the length of time between surgery and chemotherapy for other patients. Along with the surgery and the treatments, the hard work, planning, and organization had paid off. Test results revealed no cancer.

❖

The trip was one of those dream vacations in which it seemed everyone worked at making it special as they celebrated the end of a hard-fought battle. As always, Joan had the trip well-planned. An article in *USA Today* advised early arrival at the park to be ahead of the crowds, a break in the mid-afternoon, and then a return to the park at night. That suited her fine.

Each morning they rose early, ate breakfast in their room, got to the park before it opened, and were able to get into the exhibits without a long wait. The afternoon break allowed Joan, who still tired easily, to nap while the boys swam. Too soon their time at Disney World ended, and they packed up and headed for Jim's parents' home in Florida where they planned to spend a few nights.

Roberta and Glenn Henderson had retired years earlier and moved to Florida. When Jim had called to tell them of Joan's cancer, they had offered to help in any way that Joan and Jim wanted. What had worked best was their keeping in contact with Jim weekly by phone, listening to him. Just being able to share his week with them had been a tremendous help to Jim.

As the family headed to Roberta and Glenn's home, a storm closed in, and as Brian drove across the nine-mile span of bridge between Tampa and St. Petersburg, hurricane force winds pushed the car while mountainous waves crashed against the bridge. "Why are you letting him drive?" Brent demanded. But there was no stopping on the bridge. Everyone's eyes were glued on the road. "You can do this," Jim encouraged his son who was driving with a learner's permit.

Just as Brian needed encouragement when facing new situations, he was able to offer it to his mother. One afternoon, facing new tests and wondering what the results would be, Joan began to struggle with anxiety. Brian put his arms around his mother and said, "Mom, you have to count on it being good until they tell you that it is not good." Great advice at any age, and it was the handhold she needed.

The boys had helped to carry both Joan and Jim through the tough times. Their activities had kept the family involved in living.

Brent had grown from a little boy into someone interested in athletics and he was having a good deal of success with them, especially baseball. School and his "Search" program for gifted students was a bright spot in the week. His Search teacher's interest in him and efforts to help him cope had kept him confident and outgoing.

Brian was now noticeably taller than his parents and he loved to tease his dad about his height. He had become a young person willing to shoulder responsibility at home, quietly doing extra chores without being asked. He too loved sports and had begun to narrow his focus to baseball.

And they had demonstrated their willingness to be present to their mom. Brent found fulfillment by running to get things for his mom, fixing her food; Brian would sit with her, rubbing her back, holding her hand.

Facing each day as the only one they had and making the best of every moment had paid off. That did not mean there was not a time for sharing what a lousy day it had been or that Joan was hurting badly or her family was hurting. Those feelings were shared too, talked over, and effort was made to correct whatever was wrong or to help each other over the hard spots. Families of both boys' friends had recognized the need each child had to take a break during heavy treatment times and let them know that their homes were always open to them.

"Everyone has their difficulties, it's just that cancer is ours. We're either in charge of the situation, or it is in charge of us. Right now, we are in charge," Joan said. "It's hell what it does to our family, but it will make our boys better friends, betters lovers, better husbands, better fathers because they have experienced this. I wish it wasn't happening to me or to them, or to any of us. But it is. That is reality."

Joan's family and others too were learning from her. Instead of staying wrapped up in her own problems, she continued, although at a somewhat slower pace, with the activities she had always done. She reached out to new cancer patients with letters. When a friend had surgery, Joan went to the hospital and sat by her bed until she made her laugh. Then she went home and prepared a meal to be delivered to the family. While Barb was working, her daughter had a serious bicycle accident. It was Joan who cleaned the girl's wounds and comforted her while Barb was enroute to take her to the emergency room.

She participated with Jim at the handbell choir's annual ham luncheon in November. Jim was at the church at 6:30 a.m. with the other choir husbands to begin preparing the meal while their wives got ready to play for the service that morning. When services were over, Joan stationed herself at the door to collect donations that would pay for new choir robes. Church members quickly got the idea from Joan's appearance that a $5 or $10 donation was not what she had in mind. She had tucked $20 bills through the shoulder straps and across the bodice of her jumper.

❖

As Christmas neared, the Friendship Class began their annual hunt for a home large enough to hold the Christmas party for sixty or more persons the first week of December. Joan, back in class now that her radiation treatment was complete, raised her hand. "We'll do it," she offered.

Suddenly everyone who had not wanted to host the party began to volunteer. "It's too much for you Joan," someone said. "I'll do it."

"Sorry, I was first," Joan said. "Put her down for next year." She would not be swayed. Joan needed control to feel worthwhile. She needed the power to make a decision and take action when she could. The class, trying to protect her from overdoing for the party, was forcing her into a role she did not want. Allowing her to be the party host told Joan that the class still saw her as competent and capable.

The night of the Christmas party was cool and crisp. Brilliant white stars gleamed against a black winter sky in majestic contrast to the splash of color from the sparkling Christmas lights. The sound of a piano playing *Silent Night* drifted out to greet each arriving guest as the front door swung open. How serene and peaceful the world seemed.

As members of the class arrived with covered dishes Jim, looking happy and rested, directed them to the kitchen where Joan peeked under foil, oohed and aahed, and said something like, "This looks wonderful . . . where do you buy stuff like this?" She ordered desserts to one room, main dishes to another. As she tossed greetings and wisecracks at guests who returned them with relish, she soaked up the pleasure of having people in her home, savoring each moment. How right she had been to insist on hosting the party. It was one more example of the patient having the best information on her needs.

After a huge dinner of ham, fruit salads, vegetable salads, green beans, a half-dozen sweet potato recipes, and desserts that it seems only church members know how to make, the class sat down to their annual gift exchange.

The laughter was brighter that night somehow, and the antics more incredibly ridiculous as members showed off their gifts. Charlie was the group commentator, wearing his pink visor with a sprig of mistletoe attached to a spring that waved back and forth. Giant, ugly ashtrays, flowered undergarments, farm tools, and Christmas bulb earrings were all cheered and applauded as each guest unwrapped his or her gift and held it up for all to see.

It was good to be alive and surrounded by friends. It was the first time since her diagnosis the whole group had been together. A kinship had grown up around Joan and Jim and the class and such a feeling of warmth covered the gathering that class members found it hard to leave at the end of the evening. Joan, seated on a tall stool, radiant in a turquoise silk blouse that set off her deep blue eyes, brought pleasure to those who had watched her struggle. With Jim, relaxed, standing at her side, it was difficult to comprehend how much pain had bought this moment. It was a scene the class needed to see, wrapping up almost at a glance the faith that she lived and clung to.

She summed it up this way in some notes that she sent to her college newspaper.

Faith is a very personal thing to me. I draw on it constantly and feel that without God I would have lost my sanity months ago. My faith gives me strength for each day and the courage to face the truth without fear. I don't think that I am afraid to die. I just want so very much to live.

I have had some definite thoughts about religious concepts. I'll share them with you. Don't forget, my faith is a pretty basic, dirt-between-the-toes type faith. I cannot quote scripture or even justify my beliefs. It's just me and where I am with my God.

I've had some well-meaning people tell me they will pray for me and that we must accept God's will. This is not God's will. God loves me. He does not want this to be happening to me. God is not a monster. He has promised He will be with me always. He will be my strength and my refuge. God does not torture people with sickness. Perhaps that is why I seldom feel the "why me" question. It just plain IS. To blame God is to go against the very nature of God as we know Him in Jesus Christ. The cross of Calvary says to me that God is in this with me, not a bystander. You see, my God hurts when I hurt, and He cries with me, and He gives me so much love that, if I will accept it, I will find the strength for each moment.

I hope that you can tell that I love God and try to follow Christ. But when people say we must pray for a miracle, I'm sure my face tightens and flashes TILT-TILT! It's not that I don't believe in miracles. I just see all healing as a miracle of God. It's very hard for me to believe that God would arbitrarily pick me for a miraculous cure. God could work me as a miracle, He's God. But I don't think He should unless He plans to take care of everyone's hurts. I hope I have explained this right. For, I do believe in miracles, and I'm reassured that all of life is a miracle when I look into the faces of our boys. We have but to look. Miracles are everywhere.

Joan had been in treatment for almost a year, and throughout that time relationships between the Hendersons and their neighbors and classmates and friends had deepened. For all who knew them, that Christmas remains marked by a special closeness that can only come from knowing how fragile and how precious life is.

❖ *Nine*

A January winter storm was soaking Nashville, turning it gray and gloomy in sharp contrast to the sunny skies and balmy temperatures of the Florida vacation several months earlier. Then Joan was well, the outlook was bright, and it seemed that the family had reached the solid ground Joan had written about in her diary exactly a year earlier:

> Simple acts of hope kept Noah focused on the possibility of solid ground. I will keep hope. There will always be times when I must wait on a storm in my life. I have a choice. I can wait in despair or I can make acts of hope and remain confident that dry, solid ground is ahead. I know it is!
>
> Change takes place when things are 'shaken up.' This challenge of cancer is God's way of preparing me for something new and wonderful. God, out of this chaos and fear, I will find Your new beginning. Stay close.

Now, even the weather signaled the coming storm. It was an ugly day for ugly news. A heaviness in her chest, then heart pain that would not go away sent Joan and Jim back to Nashville Memorial Hospital. By the time they arrived, Joan had gone from discomfort to serious pain. As Jim waited in the emergency room hall, Dr. Miranda, Joan's oncologist, passed by. To Jim, things seemed calm and in control. "Joan's being checked," Jim began when Dr. Miranda asked why he was there.

The physician immediately left Jim and went to see what was happening. As Jim watched, Joan's doctor barked, "We've got a critical situation here!" sending a cold dread through Jim. Joan's room filled with nurses and doctors working on her.

Watching helplessly, alone in the hall, Jim thought, It's happening right now. This is me, and my wife is dying. They had talked about the possibility of her living only twenty more years instead of forty more. He had always thought, Her condition is bad but . . . . It was the first time he prayed, God, don't let her die.

Quickly he went to find a telephone.

Today was Cheryl's day off, but she had come in to finish up some paper work. "I'm coming," she said when Jim told her he was in the emergency room.

Test results from nearly a gallon of fluid taken from Joan's lung in an emergency procedure initially tested cancer free, and hopes ran high that Joan was okay.

Cheryl cautioned them to wait until the final tests to tell the family. Every time before, preliminary tests had shown cancer free.

Cancer. The final tests showed cancer cells in the fluid. The elation and relief that came with the first results were replaced with the crushing news that Nashville Memorial had nothing left to offer. Experimental chemotherapy was Joan's only hope, if Nashville's Vanderbilt Medical Center or another experimental cancer center would take her, and if the cancer had not spread to her bone marrow.

"I think you need to take a deep breath and think about it," the oncologist said before leaving them alone. "This is getting pretty harsh."

A pall hung over the room as Jim stood staring out the window with Cheryl by Joan's bed—all three lost to despair as the doctors departed.

Almost immediately there was a tap on the door, and a hospital executive Jim had befriended walked in. The executive had no way of knowing the Hendersons' tragedy, he had come for a brief, friendly visit. The man's wife had been diagnosed with lung cancer some months back, and Jim, alerted by Cheryl of his struggle, had spent a lunch hour with him just listening.

Seeing that something was obviously very wrong, he said, "Let us have a word of prayer if that would be all right." After praying briefly, he hugged Joan and Jim and left, never asking for a word of explanation or detail.

Jim and Joan had pinned their hopes on conquering the cancer the first time. Just then, they felt they had nothing left to give. Their money was gone. They were tired. They had a couple of good months after nearly a year of treatment. The reoccurrence had come so quickly after the last treatment, there was almost no time to bounce back. Their emotional, physical, and financial reserves were exhausted.

Joan looked pale and tired against the white sheets. "How can I ask our friends to support us, to help us again?" Joan asked Cheryl. "How can I ask you to do this again? How do you begin to ask? Do I stop here and get a few good months?"

Cheryl knew her friend had every right to stop treatment, but that was a decision only Joan could make. "You lead and we'll follow," Cheryl said, taking Joan's hand. Her answer gave Joan the permission to decide either way.

The next day as Jim walked with Cheryl down the hospital hallway, he asked, "What were you thinking when you left the hospital last night?"

"Where are you, God, in all of this?"

"I was too."

❖

That night Joan and Jim began making new plans. If she was accepted at Vanderbilt, they would call Joan's mom and ask her to come to Tennessee for a while. They would put in a request for Joan's experimental chemotherapy to be administered on Fridays so Jim could spend the weekend with her while she was at her worst. They would redo Jim's work schedule to cut back on his travel. They had to arrange rides for the kids with ball team parents. The decisions they were making were only for the most critical needs; they were too burned out and overloaded with life and death decisions to think creatively about anything else.

As they were talking, several well-meaning visitors arrived, talking in athletic language. "You need to pull together, this is a team effort," one man said.

Jim looked at him blankly. Although he had coached much of his life, he could find absolutely no connection between fighting cancer and sports. The comment only served to make him feel more removed and isolated. Cancer and athletics were not even in the same universe.

Others came too, seizing a break in the conversation to offer solace, "I know how you feel," someone said. But no one knew how Jim was feeling, although he wanted to tell them just to let off some steam. They did not know how it felt to hold Joan as she cried herself to sleep night after night. They did not know the crushing pressure of bills that never ended, sucking away college funds and life savings. They did not know what it was to cry every morning in the shower as he looked into a future that might not hold Joan in it and saw their children without a mother. Nobody in the world knew how horrible he felt. To be allowed to tell someone would have helped release some of the stress.

The day after Joan's heartbreaking news, Curt, a regional sales manager for Jim's company, called Jim at the office on business. "How are you doing?" Curt asked.

"Not good," Jim answered. He did not follow his usual custom of adding, "But things will get better." Everything was crumbling. Joan was bad and the financial problems were beginning. He had checked his insurance policy and experimental treatment was not covered.

"See you later," Curt replied, catching the change in Jim's tone. Although he had a tremendous travel schedule, he caught a plane from Iowa to Nashville, arriving at the office later that day.

"What are we working on?" Jim asked, noting Curt's missing briefcase.

"Nothing. I just wanted you to know we will do whatever we can to support you in this," Curt said, then expressed a number of personal messages he had collected from office personnel at the main office. The two men later went to lunch, spent part of the afternoon visiting Joan, and attended Brian's ball game.

Later, his Pella work friends sent notes and called, giving Jim an opportunity to encourage them to call Joan too. "Really, she's easier to talk to than me," he told them.

Don and Cathy dropped by the hospital too, and while Cathy and Joan talked, Don asked Jim, "How are you doing?

"Things are out of control," Jim answered. "There are so many different doctors, laboratories, clinics, and specialists sending us bills and filing insurance that it's impossible to keep up with. Now, we'll have even more from Vanderbilt."

Don, an analytical thinker, listened to what Jim was saying without charging in with a solution. He began sentences with, "Have you thought about this . . . . Here's something I have done . . . . Other people have done this . . . . " As Jim responded, Don began to develop a solution for Jim's need to create order and control in the paper flow part of Joan's illness.

Don and Jim decided to keep track of insurance payments and medical bills in a large collapsible file. Each bill was filed in chronological order by its individual business name. Vanderbilt had one file, Nashville Memorial had another, each doctor's bill was also filed separately with a name on the tab of each separator. When an insurance reimbursement notice arrived, Jim stapled it to the corresponding bill using invoice numbers as a reference. Although he could not always pay the bills, being organized and having them in order and under control allowed Jim to feel competent.

Later, while sitting with Joan at Vanderbilt, Jim brought the bills and the folder and spent the long evenings stapling payments and keeping the file up to date. Without Don's advice, Jim could have contacted his insurance company or the hospital business office to help him create a system.

Although hospital finance departments can help get bills organized, when long-term illness occurs a financial planner should be consulted for the best possible use of funds.

Along with finances, Joan realized that it was time to begin to get legal documents in order and signed. "I know you know how to get a living will signed," she said to Cheryl. "I don't want Jim to have to do it." Cheryl got the documents needed from the admitting office and made sure that it was filled out correctly. From then on, Joan carried a copy in her purse and made certain a copy was attached to her medical chart.

Betty, Brother Ben's wife, had felt an urge to stop in and see Joan before she was released from the hospital.

"I'm so glad you came by," Joan told her. "I want you to write down what funeral service I want and give it to Jim. You'll need it if I die." She had written out the scriptures, songs, and names of the pallbearers she wanted. "Make sure Fig sings *More Than Wonderful*, that describes my feelings."

Betty sensed Joan's relief when everything was planned and out of the way. She had been a widow and knew the burden Joan's planning would lift from Jim. She had offered help at different times, "I have a schedule that allows me to meet kids." She had shown herself a willing helper and while Joan had chosen her for a difficult task, it was one she understood.

"I know you will hold this in confidence. I don't plan on needing it soon," Joan told Betty. "I don't want to appear morbid and make Jim and the boys think I will die soon."

Later, Joan's sister Debra came to visit and helped Joan finish her funeral arrangements. Debra had worked at a funeral home in Iowa and could help Joan plan visitation, services, and preparation of the body, thus relieving Jim of the burden of those decisions. Then it was done and the information put away.

❖

Joan had gotten increasingly better since her last radiation in September. She and Jim were back at church and Sunday school regularly, joining in class projects and socials. Members of the Friendship Class had rejoiced when Joan did just what they knew she would do all along—beat the cancer. The majority of the class had participated in her healing through prayer, food, gifts, visits, and doing chores.

"Joan's just been released from Nashville Memorial, the cancer is back," shared the appointed liaison Sunday morning. "Her only chance now is experimental chemotherapy at Vanderbilt Medical Center. They've checked, and there's no cancer in her bone marrow, so she'll be going to Vanderbilt soon for a bone marrow harvest, then check in for six weeks of intense chemotherapy."

The news hit the class hard. Joan had fought her first fight with cancer as though she was training for the Olympics, and now it was back. Each week in class and in small clusters, the family's struggles and ideas for helping were discussed. Instead of being just a Sunday school class, the group had become part of the Hendersons' extended family.

Now they were seemingly back at square one, except that instead of climbing a mountain, they were facing a sheer cliff. Most things in life are temporary—a broken leg, trouble at school, financial setbacks. If you hang on long enough those things will pass. But now, along with Joan and Jim, the class was faced with the fact that Joan's cancer was not temporary. They were reminded too that death is not temporary. The class was coming face to face with its own mortality through Joan.

Where did the class begin again? Through constant feedback from the Hendersons that what the class was doing was right and through continuous sharing of what was going on with them, it was clear the class's support was important and valued.

"Parking at Vanderbilt is going to cost Jim a fortune," volunteered someone who parked at the hospital.

"Think about it, parking seven days a week for seven weeks at about $6 a day, it comes out to $294," said the accountant in the group.

"Add food for Jim in the cafeteria, the cost of driving down there and back everyday, taking the kids out to eat, it's a small fortune," added someone else.

"Let's take some action," the class president broke in. "Do I hear a motion?"

In quick order, the class voted to collect money to be given to Jim to use for whatever expenses he encountered. A basket was passed immediately and $300 was collected. Cheryl R. and Mike agreed to take the money to the Hendersons along with the dinner Cheryl was preparing. Perhaps it would send a message that they still had solid support from their Sunday school class.

Cheryl promised to report back on any additional news after visiting with the family. Members who wanted an update could call her instead of intruding on Joan and Jim's family time as they prepared for her next treatment.

When Mike and Cheryl arrived, Joan was sitting at the kitchen table watching Brent and a friend playing in the backyard. Jim was fielding yet another telephone call from anxious friends who had heard of Joan's cancer reoccurrence. Jim excused himself from his caller and sat down with them at the kitchen table.

Mike produced a little bundle of money, "You're going to need this for parking at Vanderbilt," he said, handing it to Jim.

"Parking won't be such a big deal," Jim said. But later, when he began going back and forth from work to the hospital two or three times a day, parking costs jumped to $10 to $15 per day.

Joan was looking great, even feeling good. She looked so good that Mike shot Jim a questioning glance.

"We keep thinking they've got her records screwed up," Jim said. "She has been feeling better and better. Then she got the fluid on her lungs, and we were convinced that was a reaction from the radiation. She was just feeling so good, and so mentally and physically on top of it that we wanted to say, 'There's got to be something wrong here. Do you have the wrong report, the wrong diagnosis? She feels so good.' I guess that's the mental defense of knowing the treatment is so awful."

"What are the doctors saying about the treatment?" Cheryl asked, following up on Jim's opening. With more information she could help the class decide on additional types of helps.

Joan explained that she would be dangerously sick with no immune system so visitors should not come. "They say the treatment can kill or possibly cure me. It just makes me so mad! I will not let it get ahead of me!"

Another action the class could have taken was to investigate other parking opportunities. Eventually, Jim did discover a free hospital parking lot one mile from the hospital that was serviced by a shuttle bus. It became an enjoyable break from routine to ride the shuttle or walk the mile to the hospital. An added bonus was that the shuttle drivers created a *Cheers* syndrome—a place where everybody knows your name. The drivers remembered him and asked about his wife when he jumped on the bus.

A second way the class could have helped would have been to provide a book bag to collect current magazines for all members of the family to read while at the hospital. A bag could be placed in the Sunday school rooms so that other classes could participate in sharing magazines they had already read. A person could be designated to take the magazines to the hospital each week.

Finally, a telephone answering machine could have been furnished. The machine could have recorded calls while Joan rested, informed callers of Joan's current condition, and allowed the family to get "thinking of you" messages without having to interact on a tough day or miss family time while answering the phone.

The next Sunday, Joan and Jim sent a note to the class:

Dear Friendship Class,

So much has happened in the last ten days. We've had a rather major challenge thrown in front of us again. Frankly, we're a bit weary. Last Sunday we were really struggling to put our feet back under us when Cheryl and Mike brought new substance to draw strength from.

Yes, the dinner was great, and we do so appreciate your constant support, but the love gift was a gesture of unmeasurable worth. You were recognizing our needs before we had even gotten that far.

Your words of encouragement and unconditional love help us realize we can start again. It doesn't matter that we are weary. You have told us that you will be there to reach down and pull us up—to shove, push, or gently kick our backsides forward.

We need you and find great strength in your friendship and love. It's a new day. We move forward in faith.

Love,
Joan and Jim

❖

There is strength in friendship and love, but Joan's medical bills were stacking up, and the Friendship Class and others wondered what other ways they could offer to help. When Joan's treatment was finished, the insurance paid only eighty-one percent of all costs. Add increased food and travel expenses and less time for Jim to work, and it was becoming clear that Jim and Joan could not withstand the expense without help. They were not going to quit trying to get Joan well. The Friendship Class knew that it was time for the church and the community to share in new ways, including finances. But how could the class ask?

One way is to approach a friend close to the family and voice concerns. Ask, "Should we be concerned about medical costs or food costs?" Do not go to an employer for information about a patient's finances or insurance.

A church member Jim knew well appeared at the Hendersons' door one day and handed him an envelope with twenty-two bills—all $100's. "A friend and I have been talking, and unless you're independently wealthy, you need this," the man said. "This is a gift, but I'd prefer others don't know the donor."

When Jim learned the other donor's name he went to his office to thank him, but the man said, "You don't need to thank me, I should really be thanking you for the opportunity to help you. I've wanted to do something and I'm glad for the opportunity." And that was that!

When Jim left he thought, I imagine he really did enjoy that, and felt good.

Nancy and Joan had met shortly after the Hendersons moved to Hendersonville. Members of the same church, the two also shared rides to Nashville to P.E.O. meetings and later worked together when a new chapter was formed in Hendersonville. As cancer treatments progressed, Joan continued to attend P.E.O. meetings whenever she could. After the meetings she shared in an upbeat, factual way the problems and concerns she had with her cancer treatments. "The last time I was at Nashville Memorial, the receptionist said she could hardly bear to charge me for the treatment they had done," Joan said one time.

"How much was it?" someone asked.

"I don't know, she didn't want to say. Besides, what difference does it make? I've got to have it."

Just by listening, class members and friends were able to pick up clues to the family's financial strain. The boys were not going to get their usual Easter treat, passes to Opryland, a Nashville theme park. Winter was changing into spring, and the boys had grown out of their clothes; more purchases were squeezing a budget hit hard already by medical bills. Replacing a heating and air conditioning unit that collapsed during the previous summer's heat wave had dealt another blow to finances.

Members talked among themselves about offering financial help but were reluctant to do so for fear of offending Jim and Joan. How do you hand someone a twenty-dollar bill and not embarrass them or yourself? As a nurse, Nancy was aware of the tremendous medical costs the family was bearing, and after discussing it with fellow club members and her husband, she decided she must talk with Joan.

At about the same time, people at the church began to approach Jim's friend Don, asking his advice on beginning a fund and Jim's possible reaction. Don knew Nancy was making inquiries about starting a fund at a local bank and sent those persons to her.

Members of the Friendship Class were thinking of a fund too, in addition to the love offerings they planned to collect. Bettye, an officer at a local bank and a class member, told class members she had been approached by Nancy to gather fund information, and so the class voted to pursue the fund through Nancy and support her efforts.

Nancy knew that the concern of the Hendersons' friends were for Brian and Brent as well as with Joan and Jim. She also knew the feelings of the boys would be of major concern to their parents in accepting a fund. She would have to make the offer in a way that allowed Joan and Jim to refuse it without feeling guilty. First, though, she would find a time to talk with Joan in private.

The time came when Joan was alone at home and well enough to talk. Nancy was very direct. "I understand you have a lot of medical bills that aren't going to be paid by insurance and more to come because of the experimental treatment," Nancy said. "There are lots of people who want to do something financially for you, but it's difficult for them to know how to do it. Will you speak with Jim about how he feels accepting money from a fund?"

Joan stared at Nancy. "I can't believe so many people want to help," she said.

"It's true," Nancy assured her.

"There are so many people already helping, to ask them to help again . . . " Joan began.

"A lot of people in P.E.O. and the church who want to help," Nancy repeated. "Several people approached Don, and he sent them to me. Your Sunday school class wants to be involved. Think about it and let me know."

The next night Jim called Nancy. Joan was still quite ill, but he asked to come to Nancy's house to discuss her offer.

"Why don't we come to you?" Nancy suggested.

"No, Joan would like to get out for a little while. She would like to come over to your house," Jim replied. Nancy's home was less than a mile away, and Jim suggested they come in an hour.

It was difficult for both Nancy and her husband, Lowell, to approach Joan and Jim about the fund, although they were sure the Hendersons would understand they were trying to help.

When they arrived, Nancy showed Jim and Joan into the living room where Lowell waited, then quickly served a light dessert. Everyone knew why Joan and Jim were there, and Nancy got right to the point, repeating what she had told Joan.

Jim began to wonder, Are these people questioning my ability to take care of my family?

Lowell answered Jim's unspoken question. "If you're like the rest of us, there's no way you can't have some needs. Most average people would have a difficult time dealing with the expenses you must have," he said kindly.

The way Lowell said it, like a friend, made it sound okay to Jim, and he listened as Nancy proceeded.

Nancy had done enough groundwork through Bettye at the bank to be able to give Joan and Jim specific information. "The fund will be set up for medical bills, and Jim can withdraw money as he sees fit. Once established, Jim will have complete control of it," Nancy said.

"I know at this point that you feel guilty that you are depriving the boys of some things they need. If friends are able to help you in a quiet sort of way, maybe the boys won't have to be as aware of the financial problems, and life can be a little more normal for them. Let people in some small way relieve some of the burden," Nancy urged.

Jim thought for a moment. "I know at this point I have nowhere to turn for financial assistance. If Joan is to have treatment I know what the cost will be, and a lot of it is not covered. I want her to have a chance."

After talking a while longer, the four agreed the fund would allow for anonymous contributions. Information about the fund would be passed by word of mouth only.

Getting word to friends in Iowa was approved by Jim and done by a simple, informative letter.

> To Pella Friends of Joan and Jim Henderson:
>
> Joan and Jim Henderson are dear friends of yours and of ours! You are aware of Joan's condition and the enormous expense of her treatment. We don't think that the tremendous burden of financial debt should be added to their current worries. It has already taken a financial toll on the family, and we don't want it to be more.
>
> The friends of the Hendersons have been accepting donations on their behalf. We thought you might like to join us in assisting them in this time of need. We would appreciate having their friends in Iowa join those of us who have benefited from Joan's continued life and faith.
>
> If you would like to help, checks should be made payable to Joan and Jim Henderson, Special Account, and sent directly to . . . .

Bettye had been searching for a way to help Joan and Jim and agreed to be responsible for listing the bank fund deposits—just the names and addresses, so the family could acknowledge the gift. Through the fund Bettye and Jim became friends, chatting at her desk after he did his banking. Later, Brian also came to visit with Bettye, pecking on the window behind her desk and developing his own friendly relationship with her.

Don designed a simple thank-you note.

The friends of Joan Henderson wish to thank you for your contribution. We know how much it has meant to the family.

As soon as Joan is home from the hospital, and is up and about, we know she will want to thank you personally.

Meanwhile, we wanted to let you know how much your contribution meant to Joan and her family.

The Friends of Joan Henderson

Initially, the fund was a source of both stress and relief. Stress because it reminded Jim he could not shoulder the financial burden alone. Relief because he realized he was not alone, that people did care, and that he could start a medical bill payment schedule, thus taking away that worry.

A letter from Ken Weller, past president of Central College and a faraway friend who needed a way to help, put the fund into perspective for Jim. Through Jim's tenure as a coach at the college, Ken knew Jim as a person who set high goals and pursued them relentlessly, taking deep satisfaction in his successes. He knew that for people such as Jim, the burden of charity does not rest easily.

Ken sensed that Jim would not take help without exhausting first his own personal, physical, and financial resources, perhaps to the detriment of his health and general family welfare. He knew that Jim would not spend frivolously when others were contributing to his budget, so along with a check to the fund he sent two smaller checks, one each for Brian and Brent, with clear instructions to spend it for something they wanted.

Dear Jim,

I am very sensitive to the fact it is difficult for a person who is self-reliant by nature to accept help from others. It takes one to know one!

On the other hand, as a person who spends a major part of his life arranging for people to give money away, I have learned unequivocally that many people genuinely want to help others. It sounds trite to say it, but that does not diminish the truth of the fact that facilitating gifts does not intrude on givers but rather enriches them.

From that perspective I want to thank you for cooperating with the simple and direct way your friends in Tennessee have provided for us to help. Shirley and I have sent them a check and are very happy to do so.

In addition, however, I have enclosed a separate check for your sons. I'm sure that you have misgivings each time you spend something for pleasure in present circumstances fearing it will appear frivolous. Please help them to spend it on something frivolous for themselves and chalk it up to a return, much delayed visit from a guy in a red suit and Mrs. Claus who came to see them one cold winter night in Pella long ago.

> Sincerely,
> Ken

❖

As Joan and Jim began a new chapter in her treatment, their Sunday school class and individuals again felt moved to reach out in special ways. There was much to do, but working both collectively and separately all would get done, with some special surprises and new learnings along the way.

In just a few days Joan would enter Vanderbilt Medical Center, but before she went she had her own gift for the Sunday school class. From the very first she had wanted something good to come of the cancer. "I want so much to have mattered in this business of living," she had said. She refused to let the experimental chemotherapy with all its risks rob her of a chance to share what life was like knowing that she might die.

She had experience that she wanted to offer as insight, not advice. When she was struggling to deal with the dozens of persons calling her an inspiration, Brother Ben had told her, "If people can find inspiration in your reactions, let that happen. That's God working through you." The same held true for living with cancer. "This is my thing, if you can learn from it, that's good," she said.

One Sunday she opened the class in her usual glib manner, informing the members, "I've been told numerous times in the last year that I'm going to die."

She went on. "Death is a natural process of living, it's going to happen to everyone. I just haven't gone through the normal steps. In our society, we put topics like cancer on the back shelf because they are unpleasant. If you are going to be a part of life you are going to be a part of death, because death is a reality. Why do we have to put it back in the shadows if it's something as basic as eating, sleeping, and working?

"We don't talk much about death, we don't know much about it, and so we are afraid of it. It's the unknown that we are afraid of. If you will talk about some of your feelings about death with your husband, wife or kids, then you in turn will have started to prepare for something that is very much a part of living.

"What I hope will happen is that through our sharing you can begin to talk about death as a normal, everyday process. You're going to be involved with death many times through living. Ultimately, you will be involved in your own mortality.

"I think we do ourselves a disservice, and our spouse and our children a real injustice if we can't put death into proper perspective."

Then the questions began to come from the class. "What about your children? Do you worry about what will happen to them?"

"I wake up sometimes at night, and I think about things that I wish I could do or would hope I could do with the kids, but in the scheme of things, most of them are relatively unimportant. In the years that we have had together, I think they have developed a strong sense of who they are, which is what I would want to give them. You get caught up in, 'I wish I had time to travel, I wish I had time to teach them this or that.' But what's really important is that they know my love is there, and that I know that their love is there for me. It's not like I'm panic-stricken to get my life in order, because I feel like the time we have had together has been quality time."

"What have you told Brian and Brent?" came the question from someone else.

"I've talked to the boys about life and death. I'm really not afraid of dying, maybe because in my own mind, death is not at my shoulder yet. It's just that I want so very much to live. I'm really not afraid to die, because, as a Christian, death is not something I fear. But, when I am really struggling with things, I have to remind myself that Jesus was here, and he did these same things too. He knew He was going to die. He was afraid. He cried. He talked to God about whether or not he really had to do this. Those are all stages I have gone through. And the whole beauty of my faith is that He has been where I am so I know that He is suffering with me and knows the pain and the mental anguish that I am going through and helps me through it every step of the way."

Another question came from the class. "Has it been worth the struggle and pain?"

"If I can get another year, or two years, or whatever, that's what I want to keep fighting for. Life's too precious not to fight for. But that's an individual thing. I can't tell you death won't be scary for you. My faith is very simple. My faith is that God is there and He loves me so much He will help me no matter what. There have been times when physically I have felt so terrible that the thought of death is really a neat alternative because you hurt so bad you don't know if you can make it through another day. But you do."

"What kinds of things help you get through it?" someone asked.

"Something my parents gave me as a child—a personal faith that says that you just keep on keeping on and that God loves you so much that He is going to be there with you. I pray that I have given that to my kids because that is what gets you through the tough days."

"Do you talk a lot about what might happen?"

"I don't dwell on the death issue, I dwell on the living. There are no guarantees for any of us. On tough days I may stand in the shower, turn it on as hot as I can stand it, and let it wash the heaviness off. I may shed a few tears or say a few words, then I get out and go forth with the day that I've got. You make the best of what you've got."

"You seem to handle the life and death issues so well, how do you do that?"

"My mom always enjoyed each day—dew on the grass in the morning, the sunsets, leaves falling, the beautiful roses in her garden. She pointed out those things to me so that my whole life I have been blessed with seeing more in a day's time than just getting up, getting to work, getting home, getting supper, and saying goodnight to the kids.

"I have always enjoyed my days. I don't know that it is something that you can teach. I think you can make people aware of it. Maybe if they see you living it, it becomes part of their life, and that's the way they get hold of it."

Someone in the class turned to Jim who was sitting silently, watching and listening to his wife. "Joan never seems to ask, 'Why me?' Did you ask, 'Why Joan?' "

Jim thought for a minute and then answered. "I got angry at God. She has so much life. Joan has always kept it in the Christian perspective. But I was saying it. 'Why her?' I was really angry.

"It's different for everybody. And each person in our family deals with it differently, just as each of you will deal with it differently if it happens to you. But gradually I realized that's where our real strength was coming from. Eventually I went back to reading the Bible, and I read it to Joan at the hospital. It was comforting for us, it helped."

He went on, remembering. "When I told a friend I was embarrassed by my anger at God, he told me, 'God understands that anger. It's okay, and probably the end product is a stronger faith.' I wondered why, if all the faith stuff is true, then why is this happening? But if we stick with it, the Bible and prayer give us an inner peace. God and Jesus are aware of our struggle."

❖

That Sunday was the first time some members of the class had talked openly with someone facing death. Jim and Joan's candor allowed others to begin thinking about what would happen if they were faced with death soon and gave them a new perspective to think about. Jim and Joan also provided proof that serious illness need not destroy relationships or cause a family to disintegrate.

Joan and Jim would not be coming back to the Friendship Class for a long time. They had closed out a year of treatment, a year they had begun as novices. They had bent their schedules and lives around cancer treatments and cancer center schedules, but except for a few short emergency hospitalizations, Joan had spent that year at home with her husband and children.

Now she would be hospitalized in downtown Nashville, almost an hour away from home. Life would change drastically as Joan became a full-time patient fighting for her life and Jim worked to strike a balance as a father and a husband.

❖ *Ten*

Penn had searched for a way to support Jim and Joan during her illness and treatment, but after nearly a year, still did not know what to do. Something Joan said when she talked to the class made him begin to realize what he could share.

As members of the church prayed for the Hendersons and wrestled with the unfairness of Joan's newest cancer diagnosis, Penn and others in the Friendship Class continued to act on what Joan had told them during her talk. "We all have gifts," Joan said earlier that morning. "You don't have to be able to bake a pie; sending a card with a verse of scripture or just saying, 'Hey, I care,' is a gift."

Penn, a singer and guitar player on Nashville's Grand Ole Opry, had joined the class the year before. Joan was one of the first persons to help make him feel welcome.

"I really identified with what you said today," Penn told Joan when he dropped in at her home that night. "I felt I didn't have a gift, that there was nothing I could do. But after listening to you talk and say everyone has gifts, I recorded some of my favorite songs for you."

Penn stayed less than a minute, and he was gone by the time Jim got to the front door. Joan put the tape aside while she packed for her stay at Vanderbilt; but later that night, as she and Jim prepared for bed, she pulled it out and played it. "I did this last song especially for you," Penn said on the tape. "It makes me think of the Friendship Class and how we've all pulled together and how we all feel about each other." Accompanied by his guitar, he sang *People Who Need People*.

Penn could not know it, but this was at a time when Joan and Jim were searching for positive things in her cancer experience. His tape helped to fill that need. When the tape finished, Jim placed it in with Joan's other things for Vanderbilt.

❖

While Joan still had cancer, and she continued to undergo treatment, many things were changing. Entering Vanderbilt meant that the usual interaction between Joan and her friends would be drastically reduced. Still, there were common sense ways to support the family.

Joan's mom was flying in that afternoon. Maynard had told Pauline, "Whatever Joan wants, you do."

Jim was rushing to get to a meeting and planned to meet Pauline at the airport.

Barb happened to come in for a visit. When she saw how busy Jim was, she offered to meet Pauline.

"No, I'll do it," Jim said. He still was not always up to accepting help easily.

Barb's words helped him accept. "Why? I can do it. I've got nothing else to do, and she already knows me."

Others provided for additional physical needs. "Cheryl, I want to do something for Joan, but I don't know what to do," Margaret said when she learned of Joan's cancer reoccurrence. Joan had demanded that Margaret have a small lump in her breast checked soon after she herself had cancer surgery. Margaret had undergone a mastectomy when the lump turned out to be cancerous.

"Meet me at Dillards, she needs something to wear in the hospital," Cheryl replied. As a nurse, she knew the practical side of hospital stays.

Once there, Margaret and Cheryl were immediately approached by a saleswoman in the lingerie department. "May I help you?" she asked.

"Yes, we're looking for a gown for a friend going into cancer treatment," Cheryl said. "She has a chest tube to drain her lung, then she's going to have a special catheter in her chest for chemotherapy. She's had a mastectomy so she needs a gown you can't see through. It needs to be warm because chemo causes her to easily chill, and short for her chest tube to come out the bottom. It must button up so that it's easy for doctors to check her chest tubes, and be warm but not hot, with sleeves that are wide enough for IV tubes and easy to push up to take blood pressure and . . . ."

"Okay, okay," said the saleswoman, backing away. "When you find it, I'll be glad to ring it up for you."

Before entering Vanderbilt, Cathy and Joan began to work out details to ease Joan's isolation while she was in the hospital. Cathy always seemed to be thinking ahead, working out ways to ease Joan's way, but always talking it out with Joan and getting her approval. During these long months of illness, both Cathy and Don had become dear friends to the Hendersons. "We could set up a schedule for someone to sit with you," Cathy offered.

That sounded good to Joan. "Okay, but I need someone who is not going to get emotional," Joan replied. "Someone who can come and not expect to visit or talk with me. The doctors say I'll be far too sick to even visit most of the time," Joan said.

"If you'll make out a list of who you want, I'll take care of setting it up," said Cathy. While they talked they refined the plan. Sitters would make the forty-five minute drive to Vanderbilt Medical Center after their children left for school and arrive home before the children returned in the middle of the afternoon. Each person would be asked for a specific day each week so that plans could be made for the entire six-week stay. And anyone who even thought they might be getting sick must not come.

Joan made a list of a half-dozen persons with whom she would be comfortable. As she handed Cathy the list, Joan reminded Cathy to explain to them how sick perfume made her. Each week thereafter, Cathy gave Jim a list of sitters for the week and their telephone numbers.

Half of the people on the list worked at least part time, and all of them had teenage children. Four were members of Joan's church. All of them had been friendly with Joan before her cancer. Each was pleased to be asked.

One of those persons, Laurie, stopped by to visit Joan and Jim before Cathy had a chance to call her. Jim met her at the door. "I don't know if you will take this as a compliment or not, but Joan chose you because she doesn't mind getting sick in front of you."

Laurie smiled and agreed to try it although she was uneasy about how she would handle six or eight hours sitting with someone she did not know well who would be desperately ill. She had not spent a lot of time with Joan and wondered what they would talk about.

❖

Joan and Jim arrived at the hospital thankful for the chance she had been given to undergo experimental chemotherapy. They parked across the street in the huge parking garage and found their way to the admissions desk. When they had filled out all the papers, they were shown to a waiting room. Any minute now, we'll be taken to a room, they kept thinking as people came and went. Joan was getting tired and Jim was getting worried. When would they get her into a room? After they had waited for six hours, a young man called Joan's name.

Tense and frustrated, they followed him into the elevator on their way to the eighth floor.

"I can't wait to lie down," Joan said to Jim over her shoulder, following her guide into the room.

Suddenly Joan and Jim were face to face. He was still going into the room; she had turned and was going out, full steam ahead.

"What's wrong?"

"Of all things," Joan exclaimed. "My roommate is smoking."

Jim peered into the room, a woman surrounded by a haze of cigarette smoke lay contentedly in bed puffing away as a horde of angry nurses descended upon her.

"I'll put it out," the lady said meekly.

"No," Joan was firm. Even the hint of smoke made her sick. Once established in a smoke-free room, she and Jim had a good laugh. "Can you imagine that?" she asked Jim.

"I couldn't imagine what was happening. Here we'd waited all day for a room, and before I know it, you've walked over the poor guy who was helping."

At Vanderbilt, everyone Jim met was looking for a miracle. As Joan lay in bed at night, they could hear the call buttons going off at the nurses' station, stat codes being announced over the intercoms, and the sounds of carts being rushed down hallways. The next day a new family would move in, and the crowd that had waited anxiously outside the night before would have disappeared. The entire floor was filled with patients and families searching for a cure.

❖

For Joan, having someone she knew to stay with her each day added security and comfort. Those who came carried with them the "Old Joan" and brought her out in conversations and humor. They did not see her so much as a patient but as a mother, a wife, and a friend. They brought shared memories to entertain and encourage her.

Often she was too weak to reach for her water glass. Lifting her hand to feed herself ice chips became an impossible task. When she was awake she needed someone to get a nurse, reach a box of tissues, get her fresh water, open the bathroom door, flip her pillow over, feed her ice chips, watch television with her, or sit quietly or nap in the chair by her bed while she napped in her bed. That is all that was required; the hospital staff did all the hard things.

The first time Laurie arrived to sit with her, Joan was sitting in a blue vinyl chair, hunched over a pillow. She looked frail and weak and obviously was not feeling well. Jim had arrived at work early, gotten some things done, then come over to have breakfast with Joan. Joan ran her fingers through her thinning hair, holding up a handful.

"We may have to do something about your hair," Laurie said, putting her bag down. She had brought stationery and magazines just in case Joan slept.

"The kids call me Pig Pen at home when my hair starts falling out. It even floats in the air behind me. Would you mind brushing it?"

Laurie, glad for some way to help, began to brush and Jim, satisfied that Joan was well-looked after, went back to work. "There are some scissors in my drawer," Joan told Laurie. "Just cut it all off as close to the scalp as you can."

When Jim called later, Laurie told him, "We're doing Joan's hair. I hope you like it." The giggles from both Laurie and Joan told him things were going well, and he worked several more hours before going back to the hospital for another visit.

While Laurie brushed, Joan talked about her funeral arrangements and where she planned to be buried.

Laurie, a tall, Nordic-looking blonde whose artistic talent Joan admired enormously, found herself telling Joan about her own father's death. "My father died of a heart attack and was cremated. It happened at night and there was a snow storm. When my mom called, she was real concerned that we shouldn't get on the road that night to come home since our son was only two months old.

"I was in shock myself. I never thought about going to the funeral home before the cremation. But there is a need for someone to see that the person is dead." She thought for a moment about not having seen her father at the funeral home. "It took me longer to accept that he was gone," Laurie said.

Joan nodded. She had been reading literature that her sister Debra had sent about children and funerals and had already made her plans to be buried in Hendersonville near her children if treatment failed.

The time spent together that day created a special bond between Joan and Laurie. For Joan, Laurie's presence reminded her that others were aware she was ill and were willing to be involved.

"Nice 'do," Jim quipped when he returned later, observing Joan's bald head. Laurie and Joan broke into giggles again. "You know, you two are acting like a couple of little kids!" What a relief it was to see Joan having fun with a friend. How good Laurie was to come.

❖

As Joan became more critically ill, Jim began to spend three and four consecutive nights at the hospital. He was becoming increasingly exhausted. He was taking medicine to stay awake on the drive back and forth to the hospital, then falling asleep at work. Friends worried he was nearing his breaking point. Nancy knew Jim could not sleep well at the hospital. "Really, Jim, it might be better if you get some sleep and come back fresh," she told him.

Cathy was worried too. Finally she told him, "Jim, when you are ready to let someone else spend the night, you need to call me and let me know. I have a list of people who are willing to stay overnight."

After working all week, Cheryl began to spend some weekends with Joan, giving Jim a chance to spend time with the boys. She arrived early on Saturday afternoons so that they could have an afternoon and evening together. Then she would tell them, "Go on to church and don't come here until you've goofed off at the lake for a while." She was an expert at helping Jim feel okay about accepting her offers, saying things like, "Hey, I'm not doing anything tonight, I'm coming," or, "Thursday is good for me, just make plans to do something." She knew Joan wanted Brian and Brent to have fun, to go to the lake. By freeing Jim, Cheryl could give that to her.

The effects of cancer and its treatment had overwhelmed their personal life. Dr. Miranda had said, "Keep a normal life." Having both herself and Jim away from Brian and Brent deeply disturbed Joan. "We talked about life being normal, and now you're here all the time," she said to Jim one night.

Offers like Cheryl's freed Jim for a whole day with the boys. One day, they went to a movie, then to a Vanderbilt ball game, and then came back and had dinner in Joan's hospital room. Joan was more excited than they were, and they had something fun to share with her. Brian and Brent were lost in excitement as they relived the best parts of the movie and all the great basketball plays. Their mother seemed to hang on every word; she was experiencing life through their eyes.

Parking at the medical center was too expensive for Cheryl to leave her car in the lot for two days, so her husband John drove her. Making full use of his trip, he arranged to pick up Brian or Brent or Pauline when he made the trip and either take them to the hospital or bring them home. His weekends were filled with coaching and picking up some of Cheryl's jobs around the house. He had encouraged her to help Joan and Jim, and he willingly did his share.

To keep some balance and to release tension in her life, Cheryl needed to find some outlets too, otherwise she would not have anything left to give. She and John took country drives so she could feel life—the wind in her hair, rushing water, trees in bloom. And she pursued something she had always wanted to do. "I took up hot air ballooning, it's wonderful," she told Joan one night when she had settled in.

Joan stared at her friend incredulously. "You could get killed doing that," Joan said. "I think it's an awful idea." She pulled the covers up around her neck.

Cheryl had been tidying up the small room that had become Joan's world. She stopped and thought for a moment, then said, "I had a friend who was standing still, and breast cancer came."

Six other women came to stay with Joan at Vanderbilt. Some were nurse friends like Cheryl who could help her through the roughest days and nights, others who only needed to do the things anyone can do.

As always, Joan retained control of what was happening around her, even when nearly comatose. One Wednesday morning, I arrived for my first time to sit with Joan, wondering what to expect. Joan, Barb and I had shared a hilarious trip to wig shops after Joan's first chemotherapy. We had all tried on dozens of wigs and laughed at each other, taking the edge off a difficult day.

Another time we had spent an afternoon sitting on her couch with Barb and Diane, talking about kids, jobs, and frustrations. As I rose to leave I remembered that I needed to borrow a cup of dishwasher soap. "Brian, please pour a cup of dishwater soap in an empty butter tub," Joan called to Brian. The four of us tried to muffle our giggles as Brian searched fruitlessly through the cupboards and over the washer and dryer.

"We don't have any," he reported.

"Try under the sink," the four mothers chorused.

We could not resist teasing her. "What kind of training are you giving this kid?"

"He'll learn just like I did—when he has to," she replied.

❖

After washing my hands with the special disinfectant attached to the door, I entered Joan's hospital room. On the bed was a stranger, painfully thin, gray-faced, and bald. A computerized monitor stood by the bed; a half dozen bags of liquid hung from the pole. The bags all fed into one long plastic tube that fed into the stranger's chest. I swallowed hard and backed out the door, sure I had made a mistake. This was not my friend, this was not Joan.

"Hi, Judy, I see you found Joan," Jim said, walking down the hall toward me.

I bit my lip hard to keep from crying, sucked in my breath, and followed him into the room. If I was going to help Joan, standing over her in tears would not do. As we entered, the machine's alarm went off. "Call the nurse," Joan said, opening her eyes.

"So it is you," I walked over to her bed and patted her arm.

"I thought I heard you sneaking out," she replied.

"You were sleeping. I went to find someone who could stay awake and be polite to their friends, maybe even get out of bed and entertain them," I said.

"I look a little rough, feel a little rough," she admitted.

"Your eyes are bright," I told her. "And you're still ordering people around. That's good! Have you taken over the floor yet?" I knew that Joan did not like to be hovered over. If she needed something she would tell me. Meanwhile, exchanging barbs was our way of showing care.

The nurse finally came to shut off the beeping machine and change the bags, asked Joan if she needed anything, then left. They were busy. The speaker in Joan's room constantly came to life requesting a nurse to go to the nurses' station or to another room. They would have no time to sit and talk with Joan, feed her, or hold her hand.

As I settled into a chair, Jim told us good-bye and left. Joan seemed satisfied, told me to enjoy the day, then went back to sleep for six hours, waking only long enough to eat a popsicle. She developed a crushing headache from its sugar content, become violently nauseated, and then finally settled down to nap again.

"Look what Laurie made me," she said when she woke. She pulled a hand painted terry cloth cap from her bedside drawer. "And here, look what the bell choir has done." On the back of her door hung a pillowcase autographed with hand-drawn pictures and get-well wishes. She proudly pointed to the computer-printed banner that Brent had worked on with his class. A computerized sign that said, BLOOD PRESSURE RIGHT ARM ONLY hung by Joan's blood pressure cuff. "Brent did that," she said smiling.

As we talked, the mail boy arrived with a stack of cards and laid them down one at a time on Joan's tray. A new energy seemed to fill the room. "That one's from Ann," Joan said, spying the now-familiar handwriting. "She sends me a card every week. I've got them up all over my house. Oh, and here's one from Shirley, she writes me all the time too. Something you never do!"

"What I have to say is too incriminating, it can't be written down," I replied smartly. To tell the truth I didn't know what to put in a card and sent only one when Joan was sick.

What a delight it was to see her light up as I read each card to her. I too was learning lessons from her illness. As I read the last card I looked over and saw that Joan had fallen into an exhausted sleep. We did not talk again that day.

The next week when I arrived, several plants sat outside her door. Their flowery smells made her sick. It seemed that time stood still in this room with the machines continuing their methodical click, click, click delivering the chemicals hour after hour, day after day. On the wall was another art project from the bell choir—pictures of each choir member above a bell table with legs and feet cut from magazines. Each member was either in huge tennis shoes, ballerina shoes, clodhoppers, or some other unusual footgear. Brent had added more pictures to her walls. "Draw me something happy," she would tell him on the telephone, and he would.

Joan had changed. she was thinner, grayer, sicker. Is this what happens, I wondered. Will she simply fade away? I crept over to the blue chair by the window and laid my books down. She blinked half-awake, then tried to roll onto her side reaching for her leg.

"Are you hurting?" I asked, going to her, unsure if she would hear me.

"It's a charley horse," she whispered.

"Let me rub it out for you," I offered.

"No, that's okay. I feel so stupid."

Joan had not been a toucher or a hugger outside her own family. I did not want to invade her space if it bothered her, but I also needed to provide physical comfort if I could.

"Joan, you're a wreck," I said, not unkindly. "You've been in bed for two weeks, your muscles are in knots, and I give great massages. If you don't want to take advantage of me, that's your problem. In fact, I I'm going to go down the hall and find someone who likes massages."

It worked. "Oh, all right," she agreed with a sly smile.

The power of a physical touch brings relief and comfort both to the giver and the recipient. Joan became real for me again as I rubbed her calves, then her back, gradually working out each tense muscle. There was no food I could bring her, no way to change her circumstances, but she was allowing herself to be comforted by a friend who felt helpless—what a gift.

That night as I prepared to leave she began a tradition that lasted as long as I visited her. "I love you," she said as I squeezed her hand good-bye and promised to return in a week.

"I love you too," I said.

❖

Joan and Jim had explored other treatment options before agreeing to Vanderbilt's experimental program. Dr. Miranda had been brutally honest, "It's very tough—an awful experience, the treatment can kill you," he had said at the outset. Joan's reports had been sent to other treatment centers for second opinions. Jim had checked with other doctors for their opinions. Then, well into treatment someone said, "Did you think about treatment in Canada?"

Those words, meant as encouragement, had the opposite effect. What Jim heard was, "Do you love her enough to try every avenue?"

They began living from event to event. A short-term goals was set: Survive the chemotherapy for a six-week period. Just knowing the awful treatment would be over in six weeks, that she could be home with Jim and Brian and Brent made it bearable. Then one morning as Jim watched the LifeFlight helicopter land several stories below, an intern checking Joan's chest catheter said, "Now, when you go through this again . . . ."

"What?" Joan gasped, sitting straight up in bed.

Jim felt like he had been struck by one of the helicopter's blades. "Get the doctor in here," he said sharply. Again? He stared at Joan, afraid to talk about the possibility of again. Again?

When Joan's primary physician came in, he was flustered. "Surely we have talked about this," he began.

"No, we haven't," Joan threw back at him. She was angry. Somehow there had been a slipup. No one had said anything about two rounds of treatment.

"Her body has accepted the treatment, that's really good news. She can go home for a few days, then come back for an additional five weeks. Research shows if you successfully finish the first treatment, the second treatment is recommended and has been found to remove cancer cells," the doctor explained."

When the doctor left, Jim sat on the bed and held his sobbing wife. They were both too stunned to talk.

She had always been a goal setter but now it seemed as though all her goals had blown up in her face. Completely out of energy, she could not face the thought of another round of the devastating treatment just then. "I feel like I've run the race, gotten to the finish, and now they've moved the finish line," she cried.

"I won't do it!" she told Jim and the group that sat daily with her. Over and over she worked it out in her mind. No one argued. "I'm not doing it. I don't think I can do it."

At last she agreed to do it. No one had pushed her. "The treatment has gotten us another year. Life is too precious not to fight for," she said at last. She wrote in her diary:

> You go into a program like this fully aware that the treatment may kill you as fast as the cancer. To say I was sick is a gross understatement. I have difficulty describing those days. They tested the limits of my mental tenacity as well as my physical endurance. Eight days, of which I have no recall, were critical. My fever was high, and I wasn't responding to any medication. Jim

and the friends who were staying with me each day thought I was dying. The doctors said nothing. One day I just decided to wake up and come back.

God and I have always talked a lot, but down times intensify all aspects of life. Many, many times during white-knuckle pain, I've had to say, "Jesus, Lord, help me, and we will make it through." Pain is a personal thing. No matter how much family and friends want to help, they cannot carry the actual pain.

❖

Joan lived for the visits with Brian and Brent. She loved to see them and to touch them, to hear about their sports and activities, to encourage them, and to talk over their good times and hard times. Having them with her helped her healing. But it took Jim forty-five minutes to get home and pick them up, forty-five more minutes back to the hospital, and then forty-five minutes to take them home later. Sometimes after making the series of trips and almost getting home late at night, Joan called him on the car phone, asking him to return to the hospital. As much as three hours could be tied up in one evening just in going and coming.

"I'd try to find a way to get down to the hospital," Brian said. "Even if I just went for a little while, it was worth it. Sometimes I wanted to be there every day."

Brent too spent afternoons thinking about his mother, anxious for a visit. After school he would call to talk about his day, but whenever possible he wanted to be at the hospital rather than out doing things.

Those days of sitting together as a family were so precious because they might soon end. It was important for visitors to honor them. Most seemed to understand family time was valued above all other and excused themselves when the boys came. Others, not recognizing the intrusion, stayed, and either ignored the boys who eventually gave up and left, or included them in conversations they had no interest in. What they really wanted was to be alone with their mother. What she really wanted was to be alone with her children.

With so much travel time, the Friendship Class could have designated one driver a day to transport the children to the hospital. Once the boys were safely in the room, the driver could leave for an hour or two and then return.

Easter came while Joan was at Vanderbilt. Cheryl sat with Joan so Jim could take the boys to Easter services. Early on Sunday, someone crept up to the Hendersons' porch and left a hot-pink Easter bunny, clutching an envelope between its paws.

As Jim and the boys pulled out of their driveway, Brent spied the bunny. "It won't be anything, it's just a card," Brent said as they pulled onto the street. He had already beaten Brian to most of the Easter eggs hidden around the house by following his yearly pattern of waking early and locating all the eggs while his brother slept.

When they returned from church, Brent, always the first one out of the car, raced to the front porch to examine the bunny. "It's just an envelope," he said disappointedly. "It's not worth opening."

Jim took the envelope and tore it open. "Hey, there are Opryland passes for you guys." Summer entertainment for the boys at the theme park had just been provided by someone who knew how to listen. For the next few months, Jim could plan his schedule around their trips to the park, picking them up on his way home from work.

A July letter that was circulated to the Friendship Class and others brought the news everyone had hoped and prayed and worked for.

Dear Friends:

I resort to the handy copy machine to update you on my progress. I left Vanderbilt on May 26 after fourteen weeks of intense experimental chemotherapy. I could not move without assistance, and the smallest physical tasks were monumental. Recovery is slow, but I can now walk without bumping walls, and day-to-day activities are becoming "normal." Fresh air and HOME surroundings have done wonders for the mind as well as the body. Jim and the boys have incredible healing powers.

Our Sunday school class brings us dinner each day which helps tremendously. Family and friends seem to have anticipated our needs from food to a special fund. Even though we don't know the amount of each gift, we do know your name was on the list from the bank which means you are providing for our material needs as well as our emotional needs. What can I say? Once again, words seem so inadequate. Thank you! Cancer cannot eat away friendship like it does a bank account. You continue to pull us up and carry us forward. God has blessed us with your love.

The latest tests are encouraging. Considering they did not expect me to live through Christmas, we count each day as a miracle. You are a part of that miracle. We move forward in faith.

Forever grateful,

Joan

As Joan improved, seeing her was a pleasure for those who had watched her struggle. Cleaning and peeling vegetables for weekends at the houseboat; joking with a crowd of teenagers obviously enjoying an adult who listened and joked with them; driving to the grocery in her Bronco; sitting on the porch watching Brent play; watching a sunset—each moment seemed to hold such enormous content for her. They were moments she bought with sheer determination.

The family spent four days on Dale Hollow Lake that summer with Joan's brother, Denny, and his two sons, years older but favorites of Brian and Brent. Joan's days were spent watching her family fish and swim and water ski and tube and shoot BB's and eat barbecued chicken. Life was good.

The support group was finished helping. Life was returning to normal for Joan and her family. Cheryl R. sadly announced to the Friendship Class that she and Mike were transferring to Seattle, Washington. Vacations separated many of the supporters through the summer months but each time they met, Joan and her health were among the first topics mentioned. More and more Joan could be seen riding in her car. Summer was coming to an end, and mothers began shopping for school clothes, preparing for another year.

The days flew by.

❖ *Epilogue*

Joan heard Dr. Miranda talking. She watched his face, especially his eyes. The room was bright with lights. Everything was eerie, still, and in a fuzzy haze. Later she remembered the words, "We'll do everything we can."

It was the last of August, and an enlarged lymph system heralded the cancer's return just months after her grueling ordeal at Vanderbilt. However, instead of terror, an incredible calm surrounded Joan, and later she wrote, "I felt the immediate reassurance that God loves me so much He will be with me every step of the way."

A type of radiation for skin cancer was started with some benefits noticed immediately. Three liters of the fluid building in her abdominal cavity were drained at Nashville Memorial. Joan was now under Dr. Miranda's care again. The excess fluid made her look six months pregnant as it began to build up again.

Dr. Miranda prescribed more chemotherapy to buy her time and to give her some relief.

"In all likelihood, it won't," Joan told Cheryl's Sunday school class in late fall. She had been invited to speak about stewardship, about giving and receiving gifts. Her gift to them was her insight into life with a terminal illness. "The thing of it is, if I can keep on hanging in there, they are going to find something else that is going to help me. I've just gotta keep hanging in there. Keep on keeping on. That's what you've got to do."

"What about your family. Do you worry about what will happen to them?" someone asked.

"I was trying to pre-approve everything, clean out drawers, make lists so that everything would be organized if I'm not here. And I do want to eliminate as much of the hassle as I can of that kind of thing. That's a basic instinct for me, I suppose. But I have stepped back and watched Jim and the boys. They are very resourceful and intelligent human beings. They can read the directions on the back of a can as well as I can. I know it's going to be hard when they first start to do it. Their gravy may be lumpy the first time, but they'll learn to do that, and the stepping back has taken away a lot of that fear for me that they can't handle things without me, because they can.

"If there is anything we can give our kids, it is the belief that they are resourceful, that they are good, strong people, that they can make it, that they can do it on their own. If you don't allow them that feeling, you are cheating them. I see people cheating their children every day because they do so much for them, and they don't let them struggle. I'm getting a whole lot smarter with that now.

"We have given them a strong foundation so that no matter what happens, they know that God loves them and that is the greatest gift we can give them. No matter how lousy things get, God is never going to stop loving them and helping them."

Joan's talk lasted less than an hour. As usual, she was radiant when she got up in front of a group to share her witness. People were drawn to the entire family because of their strength and candor. But back in the car, she was completely drained. The hour had cost her dearly. The afternoon would be spent lying on the couch, fighting a fever.

❖

Behind the scenes, Cathy and others once again were supplying Joan's needs. But this time it was not because she was going to get well, but because they wanted her to spend her days doing the things she wanted. Soon it became apparent that Joan was uncomfortable in her clothing as her abdomen swelled. Nancy purchased material and made a jumper. Joan was astounded and delighted. Several weeks later Nancy delivered a second jumper made by Bobbi and a soft, patterned blouse she had chosen to go with it. Joan had wondered what she would wear when she spoke at her own church in a few weeks. Other friends mindful of her rapidly changing figure purchased large sweat suits and maternity pants.

As Joan's condition worsened, Jim needed a place to share his feelings. A neighbor's home was open whenever he needed to get away for a few minutes. Don and Cathy continued to drop in to encourage the couple, taking them out for an ice cream cone or stopping in for a coke. Marilynn and Brooks planned to marry, and the Friendship Class pre-wedding party was a welcome diversion. Telephone calls, some daily, gave Joan and Jim and their friends an opportunity to share their hopes and fears.

Judy K., the bell choir director and her husband, Chuck, had joined the Friendship Class, and Judy asked Cathy to place her name on a list of drivers for Joan. Chuck began sharing lunch hours occasionally with Jim, and the two became close friends. A chance to stay with the boys while Jim took Joan to the hospital one night turned into a special evening for both Judy and Chuck as they sat on the floor playing games with Brent, who taught them how to cut origami cranes from paper.

Joan was now making short-term plans. She felt an urgent need to get Christmas shopping done for her family, and Cathy accompanied her or picked her up. A special class ring Joan had secretly ordered to replace the one Jim had lost arrived with a mistake in the inscription, and Joan asked a friend to get it redone. A local jeweler promised the ring in a month due to the Christmas rush, but he had it ready in an hour when he heard about Joan's situation and then he refused to charge for the work. Joan wanted to go home to Iowa for Christmas one more time and all efforts were expended to conserve her energy for that final trip.

When the class learned Joan's condition was worsening, they quickly made motions to commission fellow member Rich to build an oak podium in Joan's honor. Suggestions for wording on the dedication plaque were requested to be turned in within two weeks. Rich did not know Joan well, but he was moved by the reaction of others to her. An opportunity to use his hobby to create something that really mattered brought him a good feeling.

Members would not settle for a small-scale dedication. They wanted to create a special memory for Joan and Jim. A reception with refreshments was planned along with a roast of Joan.

Joan's wit, candor, and faith had changed the lives of many of her classmates, adding new depth and perspective. They had learned the value of a personal relationship with Jesus, the beauty of a loving family, the knowledge that each person can make a profound difference in the lives of others, and the truth and wisdom in the words, "We are our brother's keeper."

Now the Friendship Class was going to tell Joan what she meant to them. A Joan Henderson Day was scheduled and the telephone committee called each member to inform them that a book of remembrance was secretly being compiled and would be presented to Joan on her day.

Class members were nervous on the morning of the event and Joan was nervous too. "What are they going to do?" Joan asked Jim as she brushed her short brown hair.

Jim was nervous too. The roast could go either way. "Knowing that group, it's hard to say. Brooks promised the class planned to keep things light." He hoped that was so.

When Joan and Jim arrived at Sunday school, a crowd of about sixty persons was waiting to greet them with hugs and squeezes. In front, Joan's blue chair awaited her. Refreshments were heaped onto plates, and then Joan was seated with Jim at her side.

Mike, the class president, handed Joan a fairy godmother's wand. "It looks more like a gong," he explained. "If someone gets too emotional, gong 'em, and they're finished. Now, let the roast begin."

Marilynn took the podium first. "In September, 1986, I was quite new in this community and knew almost no one in this church. Having heard somehow that I'd played handbells in another church, Judy K. called and told me there was one position not filled in the choir. She BEGGED me to come and play in that spot.

"With nervous reluctance I agreed. Innocently, I arrived for my first practice and filled that empty slot—as your partner, Joan dear! I did not know that first morning, but soon it became quite clear just

WHY this slot as your partner had been empty, and why Judy had to beg an innocent newcomer.

"Actually I was a perfect match for you, Tweedle Dum had been united with Tweedle Dee.

"In these years you and I have played flats when sharps were called for. We've turned pages that have flown away and, as if joined at the hip, leaned to the left to follow the music and continued to play. So that we don't over-anticipate, you've coined the new musical term 'depisitate.' We've run out of music to play several measures before the rest of the group. And though we know better, when we foul up, we almost always give one another 'the look.' And then there was our last act, playing on page 96 while the group and the congregation were on page 496 or wherever they were.

"Through it all, believe it or not, we've done some music that I'm proud of, Joan, and we've developed a personal friendship that I cherish. We've shared joys and sorrows and all the little and sometimes very large things that make up our lives.

"And, Joan, you've taught me one of the greatest lessons in my life: Never, ever, ever, ever, ever, ever, ever agree to fill an empty position in a handbell choir without asking WHY that particular space is open and who your partner will be!

"I do love you so very much!"

Wild applause and a huge grin from Joan set the tone that morning. She settled back in her chair while Jim breathed a sigh of relief. This was fun!

Scott, who had witnessed an entire congregation overcome with emotional tears at Joan's talk to them, stood up and told Joan, "Joan, the next time you plan to talk about life with cancer to any group, I want the Kleenex concession. I know we can make a million dollars and donate it to the cancer society."

Then it was Brooks's turn. "Joan, when I think of the Friendship Class I immediately think of Joan Henderson. I distinctly remember the first Sunday I attended, you were one of the first people I was introduced to. This left an indelible impression: Are all of these people NUTS? However, I seemed to fit right in. You truly made me feel a part of that group, immediately, and for that I will always be grateful.

"I also remember the great fun we had working on the abused women's shelter. How this bunch of crazies pulled that off is beyond me. Thanks to you and Jim for your help and participation.

"Joan, your wonderful sense of humor is truly an inspiration to all those around you. And while we're on the subject of inspiration, let me say the manner in which you and your family have dealt with day to day adversity of late is a true inspiration. I believe God puts people on this earth for a purpose. The faith and dignity of your family is truly an extension of the grace and goodness of God.

"Joan, you have made a difference in many lives. We thank you and love you."

Suzie's note in the scrap book reads, "There is no doubt Joan Henderson has had an impact in my life. I had totally given in to my own struggle with illness. If it is God's will that I should have MS, then so be it. Joan has shown me that it may not be His will that I have MS. But, it is definitely God's will that I fight it. As I am writing this I feel normal. Tomorrow I may not. Then I can remember Joan's courage to fight back, and I know that my fight will help me stay healthy.

"Joan's example has shown me that some of us may have a little bit more to carry in life. But God's love is always there to help us along the way."

Gene's comments seemed to sum up much of what the class felt for Joan: "Joan is important to the Friendship Class and to me. My first impression was of a calm (and tall!) person. I also got the impression of one who was confident. Joan's leadership of the class party games in the church Christian Life Center strengthened that impression.

"And now Joan demonstrates for us a faith and love that is a wonderful witness to her values. In dealing with illness, she has remained concerned, very concerned for us. Joan's sharing with us the emotions and strains of a family dealing with illness was very enlightening. I remember precisely Joan's correct observation that we too often place too much emphasis on insignificant things.

"Family. Personal dignity. Faith. These are the lessons I am reminded of when I am around Joan.

"And one more—joy. Joy of life and friendships. Joy like the ringing of a bell. Not a leaping or a weeping type of joy. But a big smile, a warm and fuzzy joy. Joan is special to us. She is the kind of person I hope to learn to emulate."

When all who wanted to had shared with Joan, the television was turned on and Penn's musical tribute to Joan was played. "Joan, your life has made me realize how much my daughter means to me," he said. The camera showed Penn from the waist up, seated on a stool, looking serious and professional in a starched white dress shirt, black bow-tie, black vest, and tuxedo, as he played *If Tomorrow Never Comes*.

"Joan, they told me to keep it light," Penn said, smiling sheepishly when he had finished the song. Then he stood up. The class roared in disbelief and howls of laughter. He was wearing argyle socks, tennis shoes and red gym shorts that closely resembled boxer shorts.

Then it was time for the presentation. Pictures of a nearly completed podium were presented to Joan with a plaque with this inscription: "This lectern dedicated November 19, 1989, in honor of Joan Henderson. Joan's example, witness, and faith are a continuing lesson for her fellow members of the Friendship Class."

Joan's sense of humor made the roast a logical and good way to honor her and tell her she was loved and cared for and that by her example she mattered in this business of living. What mattered to the class was showing and telling her they cared. The class had discovered that they need not wait for an illness to show love and caring. We can begin by saying: I need to tell you how much I appreciate your sense of humor, it really brightens my day; I really liked the way you taught the class today, I can relate to some of what you said; I need to thank you, Grandma, for teaching me to cross stitch, that was a wonderful day. Telling people how we feel about them helps them to know they are valued.

Just weeks after the Friendship Class tribute, Joan was physically too weak to attend the class Christmas party. A telephone call from the class reminded her and Jim they were missed. A love gift from the class ensured Christmas would be as normal as possible for the family.

Joan's gift to the class was summed up by Joyce. "I looked into Joan's eyes and saw my own mortality. I looked into her eyes again, and I saw my own immortality. A hope. A peace. We will all make the same journey that Joan and Jim are making, but on different roads. I will make my trip with more strength and more appreciation for the good days thanks to the Hendersons."

❖

The Hendersons returned to Iowa for Christmas—an adventure with Brian driving on icy bridges for the first time and Brent wondering why someone with more experience couldn't be the driver. The days were bittersweet, for everyone knew Joan had come to say good-bye.

During a brief stay at Sue and Jim's Iowa home, Sue could see that in Joan's weakness she and Jim had become a living demonstration of Christ's power. In a speech Sue gave, entitled "Growing Seasons of Our Lives," Sue said:

"These days of illness have tempered their faith and character as nothing else had done. These months have given them and the boys a priceless maturity, and they are spiritually richer for they truly know the strength and availability of God's presence in their lives.

"No, they wouldn't have chosen a winter experience to grow, to witness to others and glorify God, but God has used this time to assure them of His promises and show them great love. Your prayers are keeping them warm and giving them strength to endure while the North winds blow. They realize fully that friendships are one of God's richest interventions in our lives.

"And, as Joan says, 'Life is good!' and it shows. As I look into her face I see such peace and I am beginning to fully understand 2 Corinthians 3:18: But we Christians have no veil over our faces. We can be mirrors that brightly reflect the glory of the Lord. And as the spirit of the Lord works within us, we become more like Him (*AP*)."

❖

After Christmas Joan and her family returned to Hendersonville where she entered Nashville Memorial Hospital on January 2, 1990.

Again their closest friends came to stay with her and Jim and the boys. No special words were needed. A hug, a hand to hold, an embrace told all that needed telling. Jim knew that those who had been constant in their support throughout Joan's illness would stand by him and Brian and Brent. It was important for functional supporters to leave a location and telephone number with Jim so he could reach them at anytime.

As Joan's condition deteriorated, a friend was sent to pick up the boys after school and take them to the hospital. Joan's family was notified and was enroute.

Joan had been semi-comatose and unresponsive for the past twenty-four hours; her respiration and breathing pattern made it clear that her death was approaching. Cheryl had been in and out checking on Joan.

"The kids are coming," Cheryl told Joan, entering the quiet room. Quickly she straightened the room, opened the drapes, and turned on several lights, and put a Sandi Patti tape on to play. Then, she helped Joan sit up in bed, put blush and lipstick on her, and brushed her hair.

Jim went into the hallway to speak with Brian and Brent when they arrived, tearful and afraid. As he walked with them into Joan's room, Cheryl, seated on Joan's bed, said firmly, "The kids are here, Joan."

As Brian and Brent reached to touch her, their mother sat up with a force, took Brian into her bed, held him and stroked him; then she took Brent, holding him and stroking him. "Pull forward. Pull forward," she told her boys, encircling them in her arms. At first sobbing and then laughing with joy at her miraculous response, Jim and Cheryl sat on the bed with Brian and Brent and Joan as she held them a while longer, then she lay back peacefully. She was never responsive again, but now each child could come and go from her room and stand at her bedside easily. Later, outside her room they all cried, but it was a better cry.

For friends waiting with Jim, they felt the need to draw him out of the room occasionally and to suggest food or a drink for the children. Joan was getting ready to make her journey, and she was okay. Jim and Brian and Brent now had the greater need.

That night Cheryl went home for an hour, calling her church's Deacon Prayer Chain and asked them to pray for easy passage for Joan. Then she returned to spend the night with Joan and Jim. When she arrived, Don and Cathy had taken the boys home to be with them. Brother Ben, Betty and another friend stayed with Joan and Jim until midnight.

Joan passed peacefully from this world into the next early Friday morning, January 5, 1990, with Jim at her side.

❖

Later that morning Jim, Don, and two friends sat around the kitchen table. Final plans for the funeral service would be made in just a few hours. Families and friends were enroute, phone calls must be made, other calls were coming in, dozens of decisions needed to be made, food was being brought in, and people needed to be met at the airport.

Don offered to take Jim's list of persons to be notified and make the calls. He kept a list of times and locations of services. After each call he listed any messages the person wanted given to Jim and the boys.

Near the end of Joan's illness, friends had told Jim their homes were open to visitors if and when he needed them. Now Cathy took that list of persons and made telephone calls to arrange accommodations for the family. Hendersonville has just one motel, and she called to reserve a block of rooms for other guests.

Two ladies appeared and quietly took over the kitchen, careful not to interrupt the plans being made at the kitchen table. The refrigerator was cleared out and prepared for the food now arriving. They acted as hostesses—pouring coffee, making sandwiches, and cleaning dishes.

As family members arrived, close friends greeted them at Joan and Jim's home. It was a time for honoring Joan, for reminding family members how much her life had meant to those she touched. It was a time for remembering the good times and the times she spoke of her family, for picking out an humorous story she once told and then listening as the family member retold the story with an added twist. It was a time for reaffirming that she had been surrounded by others who loved her and would continue to surround her family with love.

Joan had requested a funeral lunch for everyone after the services. The Friendship Class was contacted, and Janet agreed to organize a lunch for 200-300 persons. Working with class members Sandra, Tom, and Carolyn, the other Sunday school classes were contacted and agreed to help. For a church grieving the loss of a friend, putting together the lunch gave them something on which to focus.

At visitation the next evening, friends came to offer their condolences to Jim, Brian, Brent, and their relatives. A brief introduction, a squeeze of the hand, a hug, or a whispered, "We'll be praying for you" or "I'm sorry, I loved her too," was enough.

Someone to pull Jim away occasionally to allow him to sit down and get a break, someone to help friends meet the family, extra hugs or squeezes between friends and remembrances of Joan's great faith, humor, love, and strength—all these things provided solace for those who cared for her.

Sunday afternoon services were held at First United Methodist Church. Joan's request to tape record the service for a special aged aunt who could not attend and for future viewing by her children was honored. Blank cards were placed in each pew for mourners to record their thoughts for the family if they so wished.

A poem written by Joan's sister, Debra Hutchinson Larson, was printed on the service bulletin at Joan's request. It sums up Debra's feelings and those of many others for her sister:

> Our Joan
> The Spirit of Happiness
> Fulfillment and Rejoicing
> Because of Life,
> Precious Life
>
> The Spirit of Neighborliness
> Generosity and Compassion
> Because of Love,
> Overflowing Love.
>
> The Spirit of Unity
> Support and Strength of character
> Because of Family,
> Strong Family.

> The Spirit of Praise
> Harmony and Purpose for being
> Because of God,
> Eternal God.
>
> The Spirit of Life
> The Spirit of Love
> The Spirit of Family
> The Spirit of God
> Because of Joan,
> Our Joan.

Instead of walking away after the service, distant friends and nearby friends joined together to share a meal and to rejoice in Joan's life.

Her struggle proved the truth in her words: "So much of what we do is unimportant. Please look for the joy. Don't wait to hug the ones you love and don't wait to share God's love. It's in all the little places of your life."

In a note Joan prepared for her funeral service bulletin she wrote:

My Dear Friends:

Thank you for honoring me with your presence here today. You have walked this difficult journey with us step by step. You have been God's love in action. I have not written all the notes of thanks nor even had the opportunity to speak my gratitude to some of you. Please know how much joy and peace you have brought us. I feel a sense of comfort in knowing your support will continue for Jim and the boys in the years ahead. God is so good. He loves you and so do I.

In peace,
Joan

❖

During the lunch that day, Jim looked around at all the friends gathered to honor Joan. His gaze came to rest on one and then another of them. He saw that he was surrounded by people who had showed God's love to his family.

Words don't do justice to the things we have shared, he thought. Certainly, now, the equation was different. A part of his life, their life together was over. But the gathering of friends brought new courage. These were relationships that had been built with God, with family, and with friends, relationships that would continue the rest of his life.

His eyes settled on Brooks, who seemed to know just when to visit; on Doug who had just shown up with his briefcase; on Marilynn who had such fun with Joan in the bell choir; on Lowell and Nancy who were so sensitive in understanding the not-so-obvious needs.

There was Barb, the first person he told that Joan had cancer—he had always known she would understand if he cried; and Diane, who had given sound advice and an Easter bunny, too; and Brother Ben— I'm so glad he's been with us, he has understood from the very beginning.

Across the way, there were Chuck and Judy playing with Brent; Jim and Sue who had been so supportive on the telephone; Randy, the one who made the telephone calls that made Joan laugh and laugh; Ken and Shirley—I wish everybody had an opportunity to meet a Weller family in their lifetime; and Laurie, such a beautiful person but never more beautiful than the day she cut Joan's hair.

His gaze fell on his family. Pauline and Maynard loved Joan so much, I hope their faith will bring them strength. And Roberta and Glenn, my own parents, who have felt so helpless through all of this; Debra, who helped so much with funeral preparations these last few days—she deals with funerals every day but this is so different for her, so hard; Uncle John, whose calls have been so helpful; and Denny, a brother-in-law who has become my own brother, his visits brought such joy to Joan.

Nearby he saw Cathy and Don, who spent endless hours listening; Scott, who was always ready to do whatever he could to help—staying with the boys when I couldn't make it home, helping me get a break at the funeral home when I needed it; and Judy, who brought such joy and laughter to our family—she and Joan decided to write a book. We told Joan we'd write that book, I hope we can keep our promise. And he watched Cheryl, the guardian angel who was with us every step, when Joan awoke to see the boys and when Joan died. I'm so thankful she was with me, how can I ever thank her; and John, he took over at home for Cheryl and Bettye, she made the fund comfortable; and Diana, she helped us get ready for the fight.

They all are here. It is not really a surprise to me to see them with us any more, he thought. They always seem to know our needs before we do.

❖ *Appendix*

We have tried to include in the appendix to this book some of the practical information, ideas, and materials that we came across. We hope that you find them helpful in the times and places that you and your friends, family, and church communities find it necessary to be the hands of God to someone you know and love.

The Authors

❖*Spiritual Gifts and Caring for Others*

The reason for the spiritual gifts is explained in 1 Corinthians 13:7: The Holy Spirit displays God's power though each of us as a means of helping the entire church. To that end the Holy Spirit supplies us with six spiritual gifts which, according to Dr. Charles R. Swindoll, "enable the recipient to perform a function in the body of Christ with ease and effectiveness." Swindoll illuminates those gifts in his publication *Spiritual Gifts* and we have sketched some definitions of them based on his work:

1. Leading—Possesses the ability to lead others tactfully. Able to see order among chaos, and to bring it to pass. Has a good dose of common, practical sense.

2. Exhortation—Distinct from the teacher, one who communicates truths from God's Word, the exhorter stimulates the hearer to act upon what God has said. He has the ability to "drive home" specific truths of Scripture so that the hearer is motivated to change.

3. Faith—The person with this gift has the ability to lay hold of God's promises for results far beyond the power of man to achieve. Almost without exception, those with this gift seem to have a great desire that the circumstances be "impossible. He is able to trust God regardless of how things look.

4. Giving—The ability to be sensitive to and provide for the needs of the saints with great joy and generosity. One characteristic is very prominent—confidentiality. The giver never wants to be publicly recognized, honored, or even thanked.

5. Helping—The ability to assist and support others in the family of God in practical ways, often behind the scenes, with great faithfulness and delight. Those with this gift form the backbone of the ministry.

6. Mercy—The ability to enter into the needs, heartache, and sorrow of others and to bring cheer and encouragement to the afflicted. It goes beyond the "milk of human kindness" to include an ability to know when to speak or stay silent, to be involved or to stay away and pray, to smile or weep, to agree or disagree and redirect feelings.

❖*Forming a Care Group*

Care groups can be developed in Sunday school classes or as a separate group within the church. Training and orientation is important. Information and organization are the keys to caring within the church. Members should learn sensitivity to others, communication of care, and development of relationships. We have some suggestions to offer regarding training.

1. *A Ministry of Caring* by Duane Ewers provides a ten session "skill training course for individuals who desire to become more effective caregivers in their day to day contacts, or for groups that have been recruited by the pastor or program committee in the church for more organized caring." Sessions include instruction on listening and speaking in caring ways, caring for persons who experience illness, bereavement, divorce, unemployment, and adapting caring skills. To order or receive more information, contact Discipleship Resources, P.O. Box 189, Nashville, TN 37202. Telephone 615-340-7284.

2. *The Society of St. Stephen Handbook* is an excellent guide designed to help churches create ". . . a committed band that will attend to the needs of just one needy family or person in your community . . . and then another . . . and another." In the foreword to the *Handbook*, Dr. Ezra Earl Jones writes, "Members of the Society of St. Stephen do not look upon themselves as volunteers in the church. They feel they are fulfilling their vows which they made when they joined the church. They see the entrance to the sanctuary as the entrance to the servant quarters of the House of God." Jones suggests that by following the organization's handbook, people can "become an instrument of God's transforming love."

The handbook is available by writing Discipleship Resources, P.O. Box 189, Nashville, TN 37202. Telephone 615-340-7284.

3. *The Stephen Series: Christ Caring For People Through People* is "a complete system of training and organizing lay persons for caring ministry in and around their congregations." It is available through Stephen Ministries, 1325 Boland, St. Louis, MO 63117. Telephone 314-645-5511.

4. Volunteers who will assist patients in activities such as walking, eating, bathing, dressing, and other physical activities should receive

additional training to ensure the safety of both the volunteer and the patient. Such training is available through home health care nurses.

5. Contact a social worker, psychologist, hospital social services department, or hospice to set up a workshop for members of the care group.

❖Survey the Congregation

Once a care group exists within the church, steps must be taken to determine what types of needs will it provide for and what types of assistance are available within the congregation. Do not discount anyone. While a shut-in may have needs, they can also provide for needs. Make your church community interdependent by allowing each to give and receive according to his or her needs and abilities.

A church-wide questionnaire can provide a starting point for assessing possible needs and services. Four headings will get the information you seek:

I WILL—mow, clean, visit, drive, repair mechanical things . . . .

I AM—a good listener, a nurturer, non-judgmental, upbeat . . . .

I WANT TRAINING TO—be more caring, become a better listener, discover my spiritual gifts . . . .

I NEED—someone to provide respite care, occasional visitors, help with the yard, home repairs, meals twice a week, babysitting while I recover from surgery . . . .

❖Who Is In Charge of the Care Group

While the administrator of the care group is in charge of lining up needed services, it is important that the patient and the family maintain control over selection of services and choice of provider.

For instance, a parent would like his child to be driven to and from a downtown hospital in to visit a sick parent. Provide the family with a list of drivers with instructions to check off those the family wants. Upon receiving the marked list back, the chairman sets up the ride. That way no feelings are hurt, and the family has maintained control. If you take the control away from the family, they may not allow help.

A telephone number for the support group published in the church directory, bulletin and newsletter would alert members that support is available. It also provides access to information by would-be supporters who do not wish to disturb the family or are uncomfortable making direct contact. Only information approved for release by the family is given out by the support group line.

❖Support Folder

To allow for the smooth delivery of services, a packet including types of help offered and contact numbers should be prepared. Providing a patient and family with the packet allows them to reflect on concrete offers of help. When a need arises, all the family has to do is pick up the telephone and contact the support group chairman who in turn arranges for someone to meet a particular need. Remember there is more than one way and more than one person, to meet needs—the choice is up to the family or patient. Some people may refuse help at first, but their situation may change. The support service folder stresses that help continues to be available—just by asking.

❖Write It Down

Try to remember the last time you asked someone to do you a favor. Was it easy? Did you wonder if they would turn you down? If so, why or why not? By thinking about what you are willing to offer, then writing it on paper with your name and telephone number, you let your friend know you are serious about helping.

Gather your group of caring persons together and write down all the possible short-term needs you think someone in a crisis/illness situation might have. To begin, think of things that may cause the patient or his family discomfort, then provide options for the relief of that discomfort. (Who will get Betsy to piano lessons? Who will make sure that the mail gets picked up?) With an itemized list, persons begin to feel they have permission to ask for different things.

❖*Things Your Group Can Do to Help*

There are some people who care more easily from a distance and others who wish to become personally involved. In most crisis situations enough needs exist to provide a choice for both groups.

Here is a partial list of *short-term* needs that may begin right away:

Childcare	Rides for children
Meals and snacks	Someone to talk to
Grass mowed	Mail picked up
Newspaper picked up	House checked
Pets fed, watered and walked	Ride to hospital
Someone to stay during surgery	Get medication
Figure medication schedule	Pick up family/friends at airport
Elderly in the family cared for	Sit with patient while family
or taken to activities	works or does errands

As the care group seeks to help a patient or family with *long-term needs*, these are some that may arise:

Take patient to treatment
Take children or elderly family members to hospital for visits
Include children in vacation plans
Include children in daily or weekend activities on a regular basis
Provide tutoring or access by telephone for homework problems
Provide a get away "haven" for patient or family members
Assist with birthday parties and other celebrations
Help with housework, laundry, and yard work
Rent and watch a movie with the patient
Help adapt a patient's environment—build wheelchair ramp, widen
    doorway, rearrange furniture for easier mobility
Offer to stay at family's home if nighttime emergency arises
Check on or stay with patient during day
Grocery shop
Become a "reader" of medical data and report information to patient
Read to patient

Invite patient's children to your home to create special artwork or banners for their parent

Play games with kids while parents relax

Arrange celebrations for milestones in life or treatment

Treat patient to trip to beauty parlor, barber, masseuse, etc.

Change bed sheets

Take care of pets

Assemble a swing set

Offer to attend medical consultations as a "second or third set of ears" write down or tape record what the doctor says

❖ *Instead of Flowers*

It is not always possible or practical to provide direct care to a patient or his family. But other types of useful gifts are valuable. Here are a few suggestions:

Long distance telephone certificates   Note cards

Book or roll of stamps   Tape recorder

Muscle massager   Favorite magazine subscription

Movie passes   Restaurant gift certificates

Fast food certificates   Drop off or pickup dry-cleaning or laundry

Share boat or summer home

Gift certificate for grocery store   Take car for repairs or service

Help locate employment for family members

Coloring books, crayons, or blocks for children's visits to hospital

Trip to summer, church, or day camp (provide transportation, special clothing or equipment)

Locate community resources by contacting social service department of hospital or United Way

Blank and musical tapes of upbeat music or comedy

Special treats—gum, mints, nuts, soft drinks, case of chips or boxed drinks for children's lunches

Audio or video tapes of church or Sunday school services

❖*Stress*

When diagnosis of a serious or terminal illness is being explored, the family and patient face a shakeup in their lives and normal roles within the family. While the physician prescribes "lead a normal life," the reality is quite different.

When the diagnosis is made, the family and patient may feel anger, fear, confusion, powerlessness, and even relief that they know what is wrong. Immediate, short-term plans must be made and will differ depending on the diagnosis, treatment, and individual family circumstances.

Support groups, whether informal or organized, should remember that though they cannot fix or change the diagnosis, there is much they can do to alleviate stress by offering assistance early, even before a final diagnosis.

According to Edward Charlesworth and Ronald Nathan, the authors of *Stress Management: A Comprehensive Guide to Wellness*, continued long-term stress can be devastating. Personality changes, depression, and feelings of helplessness and hopelessness can occur. "Occasionally we may feel tense and explosive. Sometimes we find ourselves compulsively repeating meaningless tasks in an attempt to control our lives. At times, we act impulsively without thinking about the consequences. At other times, we have exaggerated fears of such simple acts as leaving our house, traveling by airplane, or riding in an elevator."

The breakdown of traditional support networks is likely to cause stress and is on the upswing today, the authors continue. "Years ago, for example, the family could count on a consistent and faithful family network that would help in times of crises. In addition, we were very much less mobile, and people tended to become friendly with neighbors."

Individuals may recognize some of the stresses in their own lives but fail to see the impact of stress on others. For instance, a company lays off one hundred persons. Each will feel an impact on their income, but the jolt is decreased or increased by family circumstances. A second wage earner, substantial savings, or low expenses will lessen the stress of a lost job. Conversely, the single mom with three kids and an ex-husband who does not pay child support feels the loss of her job immediately.

J.M. Holmes and R.H. Rahe of the University of Washington have developed a list of 43 stressful events and assigned a value to each one. Surprisingly, both good and bad changes create stress. The death of a spouse is given the value of 100, the highest mean value; marriage rates 50, a change in residence, 20; and a change in responsibilities at work, 29. Any one event or combination of events is manageable. But when too many stresses pile up, life can become depressing and unmanageable.

To gain insight into the way stresses affect health, rate your stress level using *The Social Readjustment Rating Scale,* but pretend your spouse has a terminal illness. Along with the 44 points for a change in the health of a family member, add points for sex difficulties; change in financial state as treatment costs mount and you work less; change in the number of arguments with spouse; spouse starts or stops work; change in living conditions as life revolves around hospital and treatment schedules; revision of personal habits; trouble with a boss who does not understand your fatigue, treatment schedule, and/or loss of interest in your work; change in work hours and conditions as you work more, less, or different hours trying to catch up lost hours; change in recreation as leisure time is eaten up while performing dual roles; change in church activities when it is too hard to be around those who love you or you are too busy catching up or you are at home with an ill person; mortgage or loan less than $10,000 to pay medical bills; change in social activities as ill person too fatigued or not available; change of sleep habits as you are up with an ill person or too tired to sleep. What begins as no significant problem can turn into a major life crisis.

Life Event Mean Value

Death of spouse 100	Divorce 73
Marital separation 65	Jail term 63
Death of close family member 63	Personal injury or illness 63
Marriage 50	Fired from work 47
Marital reconciliation 45	Retirement 45
Pregnancy 40	Sex difficulties 39

Gain of new family member 39   Business readjustment 39
Change in financial state 38   Death of close friend 37
Change to different line of work 36   Mortgage over $10,000 31
Foreclosure of mortgage or loan 30   Child leaving home 29
Change in work responsibility 29   Trouble with in-laws 29
Outstanding personal achievement 28 Spouse begins/stops work 26
Begin or end school 26   Change in living conditions 25
Revision of personal habits 24   Trouble with boss 23
Change in work hours/conditions 20 Change in residence 20
Change in schools 20   Change in recreation 19
Change in church activities 19   Change in social activities 18
Mortgage or loan less than $10,000   Change in sleeping habits 16
Change in # of family gatherings 15   Change in eating habits 13
Vacation 13   Christmas 12
Change in health of   Minor violations of the law 11
    family member 44   Change in # of arguments with
                                                     spouse 35

Now, add the mean value scale for life events experienced in a twelve month period. Record any event no more than twice. If you scored:

0-150	No Significant problems
150-199	Mild life crisis (33 % chance of illness)
200-299	Moderate life crisis (50 percent change of illness:
300 +	Major life crisis (80% chance of illness)

It would be impossible to know all the stresses that affect those around you, and having all that information is not necessary to offer good help. Take some time to think about what your life would be like if circumstances were reversed and you had the problem.

The church as the Body of Christ can become God's hands in action, but to do so it must recognize the many sources of stress that affect people today—illness, job loss, death, divorce, to name a few.

❖Families of the Patient

Neil Fiore, Ph.D., author of *The Road Back To Health: Coping With The Emotional Side of Cancer*, is a licensed psychologist and cancer survivor. He has developed the following guide for families of cancer survivors. It has application for any major illness.

As family members of cancer survivors, we have the following rights:

The right and obligation to take care of our own needs. Even though we may appear at times to be selfish, we must do what is necessary to keep our own peace of mind so we can be better able to help our loved ones.

The right to ask for help from others in caring for our loved ones. Although our loved ones may object to the involvement of others, we must assess our own limitations of strength and endurance, and determine when we need assistance in caring for them.

The right to determine the limits of our ability to help our loved ones. By avoiding undue sacrifice, exhaustion, and resentment, we will be more genuine in the assistance we offer.

The right to balance our own needs with those of our loved ones. An appropriate balance will help lessen family tension and encourage attention to the ongoing needs of all family members.

❖Surgery and the Family

Experts say patients and their families tend to be very goal directed when facing surgery and do little contingency planning. Somewhat like jumping hurdles, the family focuses on getting through the surgery first. Once that is over they will focus on the next hurdle—getting out of the hospital.

Prior to surgery, the patient or the parent/guardian of a patient signs an informed consent form agreeing to allow the doctor to perform the scheduled procedure. This is a good time to ask for the agenda of surgery day. Knowing the agenda gives persons a sense of control and allows for planning.

Here are a few questions to ask: How long is the surgery expected to last? How long will the patient likely remain in the recovery room? When can family rejoin the patient? How long a hospital stay is expected? When are visitors allowed? What type of a recovery is expected at home (stay in bed, up and moving around, no housework, etc.)?

Patients not already in the hospital are admitted either the day before surgery or early on the day of surgery. Patients and family may wait either in a hospital room or in a waiting room with other families and patients. Waiting rooms can become very crowded so a minimum of support persons should accompany the patient and the family.

Operating room schedules change as surgeries last longer or emergencies are pushed ahead of non-emergency cases. Be prepared to spend the whole day at the hospital.

There is generally no liaison between the family and the operating room during surgery. The exception is heart surgery. Most of the time a doctor will come out after surgery and speak with the family. Any place is fine to hear good news from the surgeon. Although a private area should be mandatory for receiving difficult news, sometimes it is given in a busy hallway or crowded waiting room. Be aware that some people lose control or faint when they hear distressing news.

Remember, the outcome of major surgery or diagnostic surgery can cause anxiety for those waiting. The outcome may bring serious physical, emotional, social, and financial changes to an entire family. The family may experience sadness, anger, helplessness, or fear while their loved one is undergoing surgery. It is not necessary for a support person to fix feelings, only acknowledge them—"I hear what you are saying," not "I know how you feel."

If you do accompany the family to the hospital, we suggest that you explore the hospital as surgery begins, so that the family will not be too concerned that they will be away from the waiting room when the surgery is completed. Help them locate the cafeteria, vending machines, and the restrooms—get familiar with the hospital so you can save family time locating needed areas. And, remember each hospital usually has a chapel. We suggest that be one of the first places you visit or locate.

The surgeon gets a better idea how long recovery will take once surgery is completed. While waiting, the care group coordinator can assist the family by writing down additional concerns and questions. How long must the patient remain in the hospital? How long do you expect the patient to be off work? When can visitors come? What about long-term recuperation? Will other kinds of help be needed when the patient goes home? Will that be set up with a home health agency?

When the patient is moved from the recovery room to his hospital room someone will come out and tell you the room number. Write it down.

Who Should Wait During Surgery

At least one person (usually a family member) with some legal responsibility who can sign documents and make decisions should be there. Whenever anesthesia is administered there is risk. Decisions may have to be made about life support.

In addition, one or two clear thinking persons who can help family members keep things normal (i.e., "It's 1 p.m. we need to get some food"). These are the designated contact persons who will pass information from family to friends outside hospital and vice-versa. They will also make necessary contacts to put any of support services in place (food, childcare, for example).

❖*Two Important Documents to Take to Surgery*

One is a *living will*. A living will is a statement that tells your family and your doctor that you do not want your life prolonged by medical procedures if your condition becomes hopeless and there is no chance you will recover.

Living wills must be signed and dated in the presence of two adult witnesses. A living will can be obtained from a law library, an attorney, your hospital, or by writing: The Society for the Right to Die, 250 West 57th Street, New York, NY 10107.

The other important document is a *durable power of attorney*. A few states permit you to grant a power of attorney to make decisions about your medical care. If you grant a "durable power of attorney," your agent may continue to make decisions for you when you become unable to do so for yourself. You may grant a durable power of attorney to one or more adults, including a family member, friend, lawyer, or business associate. You may revoke the durable power of attorney at any time.

Because granting and revoking a power of attorney involve the power to manage your property and must comply with state laws to be valid, you should consult with an attorney for help in preparing the documents that will express your intentions and be accepted by banks and other institutions.

❖Waiting Room Tips

1. Patients are not allowed to eat prior to surgery—do not eat in front of them.

2. Waiting rooms can be chilly and chairs uncomfortable. Wear comfortable clothing and bring a sweater for yourself and your friend.

3. Coffee is a stimulant and increases feelings of stress—try drinking water. But if a person is caffeine addicted, it is not a good time to withdraw.

4. Gum keeps the mouth moist.

5. Bring tissues.

6. Bring pad of paper and pen for taking notes.

7. Bring quarters for telephone.

8. Ask for list of persons and telephone numbers family wants contacted. A church directory might be helpful. If agreeable to the family, provide a telephone number where updates may be provided to concerned persons without disturbing the family.

9. Strong perfumes and after shave lotions can be nauseating on an empty stomach or to stressed persons.

10. Do not bring children to the waiting room. If a family member comes with children offer to make arrangements for babysitting.

11. Do bring a book or knitting—constant conversation is draining to family members. Bring a current magazine or two for your friend.

We communicate through talking, touching, crying, laughing. But it is important not to invade someone else's space while waiting with them.

Some people while wanting support are very private and do not like to be touched. Closing in on them will make them uncomfortable. Others may want to be hugged, their hand held or to sit very close.

Here are some tips on communication for friends staying in the waiting room with the family of the patient:

1. Do not minimize the situation—"Oh, this isn't that serious, my great aunt had heart disease and cancer and she lived to be 98."

2. Do say, "Whatever you need, we'll get it."

3. Do not offer false reassurance or try to talk people out of their concerns. For example, to say, "Your wife is going to be fine, you just hang onto that!" may not be true.

4. Do say, "Whatever happens, we'll get through it."

5. Do not say, "You can't mean that," when someone speaks discouragingly. They need to voice what is bottled up. Sometimes it is unpleasant, but necessary.

6. Do not try to stop what someone wants to tell you. It takes a lot of energy to hold thoughts and feelings in. Expressing them releases the energy that may be needed for important tasks.

7. Do not tell people it is wrong to feel a certain way. They already have the feeling and telling them it is bad or that they should not have it only makes them feel guilty.

8. Do treat the family member as capable and powerful. If the family member is helpless or overwhelmed, contact a family member who can think clearly.

9. Help family see their own skills in relation to the patient's needs and new roles in the family.

 10. Do not pry. Allow the family to take the lead in discussing their situation or any problems they are having.

 11. Unless you are invited to stay, excuse yourself during medical consultations.

 12. Let the person know you are listening by nodding your head when you agree or understand.

 13. Listen and reply to the whole statement instead of interrupting or preparing a reply for the beginning of a statement. Ask questions such as, "What did you mean when you said, 'I don't know what I'm going to do about the kids?' " If you do not completely understand the reply, follow up by saying something like, "I hear you as saying you are worried about keeping the kids on some kind of schedule. Is that correct?"

15. Focus on the patient's and family's strengths and personal resources such as: friends, family, church, social services.

16. To help solve problems:

Ask: What things has you done to solve similar problems in past? What was successful? What has you done to help solve the current problem? What alternatives have not been considered?

Emphasize: The person's wisdom in seeking out help when his or her own resources were exhausted. "I think you are taking good care of yourself by reaching out to me and others for support."

List: Ideas and solutions. Persons under stress can be forgetful and distracted.

17. Do not offer platitudes such as, "God never gives us more than we can handle." Upon hearing a country minister proclaim at a funeral that God had taken the deceased home, an elderly man in the congregation mumbled, "As far as I know, God ain't in the killing business."

18. Some of what supporters hear in a hospital waiting room is confidential. Ask permission to share information so the family does not feel betrayed.

19. Be sure to write down and follow up on any offers of assistance that are accepted.

In times of crisis sometimes all that is needed is a familiar face, a warm hand, a soft shoulder, an affectionate hug. It is not necessary for you to change sad to glad, sick to well, or frightened to fearless. All that is really necessary is that someone cares.

❖Hospital Visits

"Hospital visits are meant to cheer up patients but some are so sick the last thing they need is a happy, cheerful visitor bouncing off the ceiling," says the Rev. Gary Brock, Director of Pastoral Services at Vanderbilt University Hospital in Nashville. "Before planning a visit to a patient, ask, why am I visiting?"

Some people visit because their own personal experience allows them to take something to a patient. For example, *Reach To Recovery* volunteers supply information and support to women who have had breast cancer. Some visitors represent the church and have specific training, such as Society of St. Stephen members who are responding to their own need to serve others.

This is a compilation of suggestions from Rev. Brock, Cheryl Dismukes, Mary MacArthur, and Claudia Douglass.

1. It is helpful before visiting to call first. Ask when would be the best time to visit. Remember, tests and procedures can take up much of the day.

2. A routine visit to the hospital should last five to fifteen minutes. In the car on the way to the hospital pray for the grace to be fully present for the patient and to be sensitive to his needs.

3. Before visiting, ask yourself, what is the one thing I can bring this person that no one else can? Or ask the patient, "What is it specifically you need to help you get through this crisis?" The response will be different things to different people. For example: a child delivered to the dentist, $25 a week to park, do the washing, take care of the dogs, arrange transportation for outpatient treatment, and so forth. Offer the help or help to arrange it.

4. To make such offers more palatable, say something like, "I remember when I (my father, my aunt, my friend) had surgery, people were so helpful! Do you have someone to sit with you; drive you home from the hospital; pick up Billy at school? I'd really like to help." Then allow the family and patient to talk about their disease, their situation, their story—not yours, or your father's, aunt's or friend's surgery.

5. It takes time to build relationships and establish trust. If you do not know the person well, say something like, "Tell me a little about yourself," or "How has it been for you since you arrived at the hospital?" Establish some linkages, find things you have in common.

6. One of the most important things you can do is listen. Allow the patient to look back over his life and try to make peace with parts of it. Encourage them to tell their story and then listen to it.

❖General Hospital Visiting Tips

1. Call general information for age requirements for visitors.

2. Rooms are small and filled with equipment. Two visitors to a room at a time is a general rule.

3. No smoking. The smell of smoke can cause nausea for post-surgery, chemotherapy, other patients.

4. Sick people need quiet to rest and brief visits to know that others care. Five to ten minutes is sufficient.

5. When you arrive at the hospital, introduce yourself to the nurse or the primary caregiver. Ask if there anything you need to know before visiting the patient.

6. Knock before entering a patient's room. Say, "It's Bob Smith," instead of, "Do you know who I am?" Medication can cause confusion, take it upon yourself to immediately introduce yourself to other visitors. Forgetting names can cause patients embarrassment and upset.

7. Patients are vulnerable and this is not a good time to discuss qualms or other information you have about their treatment. It can undercut a patient's trust in their medical care. If you really think the chocolate candy bar cure for cancer is a viable option for your friend, be thorough. Provide background information, names, and addresses of treatment providers so that stressed family members can make informed decisions with complete information. If you are unable or unwilling to help your friend locate the "cure," do not mention it.

8. Be sensitive about recommending other types or places of treatment; offhand suggestions can make the family feel as though others think they did not do their best for their loved one.

9. Persons undergoing chemotherapy may become critically ill. It may be helpful to offer to sit with the patient during such crisis periods.

10. Never visit if you suspect you are ill.

11. Ask the nurse which items can be brought to the patient.

12. Cologne and perfumes are nauseating to many patients. Do not wear them to the hospital.

13. Do not put the burden of conversation on the patient.

14. Do not compare illnesses.

15. If you want to become more closely involved, see what the patient is reading so you know what is going on with them. Many patients want people to know what they are going through.

16. If you do not visit well, send a card with a personal note.

Time To Leave

1. If the patient does not ask you to sit down, a short standup visit is in order. "I just wanted to let you know I am thinking of you," says it all.

2. When patients ask for pain medication, it is time to leave. Part of pain relief is going to sleep and letting the medicine work.

3. When the doctor enters, visitors should leave unless requested to stay.

4. When business office personnel come in, leave. Financial information is none of your business.

5. Anytime the nurse comes in to do anything say, "I'll just wait in the hallway," or "I'll just run make a phone call and see how the kids are doing," thus allowing the patient privacy.

6. If a patient vomits, either help, or get up and get the nurse if helping is difficult for you.

7. If the atmosphere is changing—the staff is rushing in and out drawing blood, the patient is gasping for air, etc.—do not run away. Step into the hall and wait, your presence may be useful to make phone calls or to comfort the spouse or parents.

Functional Visitors

If you would like to spend the day, first say something like, "I'm available to stay all day long if that's what you need. You tell me what you want." Be prepared to help. Let the nurse know why you are there. Make sure your presence is not a burden to the patient or the staff.

With medical staff permission, visitors can:

1. Walk the patient in the hallway.

2. Feed the patient.

3. Give a back massage.

4. Assist patient getting to the bathroom.

5. Take the patient on a wheelchair tour of the hospital.

6. Bring adhesive and put get well cards on the wall.

7. Rearrange the room if the patient is in for a lengthy stay (ask the nurse first).
8. Answer the telephone.
9. Encourage calls and visits if appropriate.
10. Encourage visitors to bring posters.
11. Help patient's children to create art for the room.

Visits to Waiting Family Members

Family members who spend long periods of time with patients also need support and visitors. Call them first and ask to visit the next day.

Any break in routine can boost their spirits and make the well spouse or family members feel less isolated. When you call, suggest:

1. Lunch at the hospital or nearby restaurant.
2. A picnic lunch or dinner to eat in the hospital cafeteria or outside.
3. Taking the family out to dinner.
4. Bringing a special snack or take out dinner to the patient.
5. Taking the family for a ride around town for a change of scenery.
6. For family members spending long nights at a hospital, suggest that they meet you late. If you are out for an evening offer to meet them at a nearby restaurant for dessert.

Death

Following a serious injury or impending death, clergymen and hospital chaplains are available and can help care for the family with grief and crisis intervention. If family has a clergy person, call him or her. If not, notify the hospital chaplain who is on call 24 hours.

Visitors can wait with the family, make telephone calls, provide transportation, make sure they get food, help make plans, and provide emotional support by just being there.

❖*Bereavement*

What should I do? What will I say? What is expected of me? What is bereavement like? The absence of answers to these and similar questions may keep some of the most solid supporters away when their affection and encouragement is most needed.

As defined by J. William Worden in *Grief Counseling and Grief Therapy*, bereavement grief tasks are as follows: to accept the reality of the loss, to experience the pain of grief, to adjust to the environment in which the deceased is missing, and to put the emotional energy that was invested in the deceased into new relationships.

Claudia Douglass, director of the Ramsey Memorial Hospice in Gallatin, Tennessee, writes in her *Grief Counseling* handout that "Grief is work!" She explains that grief is a natural and normal response to loss, a continuing process which must be experienced. Grief is based on the griever's perception of loss and is a process of adjustment rather than recovery. Douglass lists the following symptoms of grief divided into three major categories:

1. *Psychological*: shock, disbelief, depression, weeping, regression to feelings of helplessness, panic and anxiety, disorganization, anger, guilt.

2. *Social*: withdrawal behavior, appearance and grooming deteriorates, inability to concentrate or make decisions, inability to sit still (restlessness), loss of basic sense of trust, personality changes.

3. *Somatic*: loss of appetite and weight, disturbed sleep, sighing, crying, exhaustion, heart palpitations, nervous and tense, loss of sexual desire, loss of pleasure.

Ms. Douglass gives the following tips for volunteer bereavement counselors which can be used by friends:

1. Reach out to the bereaved.
2. Provide the gift of your caring presence.
3. Encourage the bereaved to talk about the actual events around the death. ("Can you tell me about what happened on the day . . . died?")

4. Encourage the bereaved to talk about their adjustment since the death. ("How has it been for you since . . . died?" "What has been the hardest thing for you?")

5. Remember that you cannot take away the pain from the bereaved— you can only help them express it.

6. Recognize that their grief may trigger strong feelings of helplessness in you. It is hard not to be able to do anything concrete to help.

7. Recognize that their grief may trigger your own memories of loss. Do not let your needs or those responses or memories become the focus of your attention.

8. Try to understand and empathize with what the bereaved is feeling. What are their greatest losses and sources of pain?

9. Show your caring. Touching and hugging can be healing. It is okay to show that you are moved by the story being told to you.

10. Do not try to explain the loss in religious or philosophical terms. Do not try to give answers, just relate to what they are feeling. ("I can see how hard it is for you right now" or "You are right, it does not seem fair or to make any sense.")

11. Do not encourage the bereaved to deny or rationalize the situation. For example, do not tell them not to cry.

12. Help the bereaved to identify the various feelings they are feeling— sorrow, anger, depression, relief, guilt, anxiety, frustration. ("It sounds like you are feeling frustrated because you cannot do anything to change the situation.")

13. Encourage the bereaved to talk about the deceased. Looking back over the entire relationship can help to bring out their feelings, and can help to eventually bring closure. ("Tell me about . . . . What were they like?")

14. Help bereaved to understand that grief reactions are normal, that they are not going to lose control or go crazy if they cannot concentrate right now or cry a lot. We need to express our grief. Only through processing it can we release it.

15. Help the bereaved to be good to themselves. Help them to find opportunities for respite and relaxation.

16. Encourage the bereaved to find new outlets and new relationships.

❖*Helping Before and After A Funeral*

Decision making abilities may run dry for the family of the deceased when so many important decisions are being finalized. Sometimes a bereaved family's closest friends are unable or do not think to help as they prepare for the funeral. The persons who have coordinated support throughout a lengthy illness will likely continue to help. If the bereavement is sudden, you may need to offer to coordinate support.

Think about things you would want done and act. Be sure to follow through and finish whatever you agree to do. Do not hesitate to ask for help, others are often just waiting for direction. Ministers are a good source of information, if you cannot reach your own, call others or the hospital chaplain. If you are not coordinating activities it may be helpful to stay in the background quietly performing your chore.

Here are some helpful offers anyone can make:

Take care of the kitchen	Clean out refrigerator
Receive food	Store food
Wash cars	Gas cars
Take suits to cleaners	Press clothing
Polish shoes	Provide airport transportation
Play with children	Prepare the home for visitors
Do laundry	Mow grass
Deliver photograph to paper	Answer telephone
Pick up papers with death notices	Host overnight guests
Call obituary to newspaper	Take children to park or movies
Write down directions from airport	Take photographs

List name and address or telephone number of funeral home, church, memorial fund, florist, and contact person for those staying in homes

Provide extra rooms/bathrooms for showers to those preparing for the funeral

Provide extra bicycles or play equipment for visiting children

House sit during visitation and funeral services

Deliver funeral flowers to shut-ins or nursing homes

Take desert trays to hospital staff who helped during the illness

Help compose and write a thank you note to the staff

Film the service

In addition, the arrival of friends and family will mean that additional food and other items are needed. The support group can help to provide:

Foods in throw away containers	Paper and plastic products
Canned soft drinks	Cooler of ice
Deli trays	Finger foods
Coffee/creamer	Coffee cakes
Cookies/cakes	Evening meal
Extra chairs and bedding	

Make certain that the family knows that whatever their wishes, they will be honored and that support is available for the coming weeks. Food, childcare, and other needs for the time after the funeral should be offered so the family knows what they can expect.

❖*Bibliography*

❖ *Books*

Aldrich, Sandra. 1990. **Living through the Loss of Someone You Love**. Ventura, CA: Regal Books. *Story of coping with husband's illness, his death, and her adjustment.*

Caine, Lynn. 1974. **Widow**. New York: William Morrow Publishing.

Charlesworth, Edward A. and Nathan, Ronald G. 1985. **Stress Management : A Comprehensive Guide to Wellness**. New York: Ballantine Books.

Davidson, Glen W. 1984. **Understanding Mourning: A Guide for Those Who Grieve**. Minneapolis, MN: Augsburg Publishing. *Talks about the importance of sharing grief. Grief is a process, and faith is a part of it.*

Davis, Martha, et al. 1988. **The Relaxation & Stress Reduction Workbook**. Oakland, CA: New Harbinger Publications Inc. *Simple directions for progressive relaxation, refuting irrational ideas, nutrition, coping skills training, time management, imagination, etc.*

Ewers, Duane A. 1983. **A Ministry of Caring**. Nashville: Discipleship Resources.

Grollman, Earl A. 1977. **Living When a Loved One Has Died**. Boston: Beacon Press.

Jevne, Ronna Fay, and Levitan, Alexander. 1989. **No Time For Nonsense : Self-Help for the Seriously Ill**. San Diego: LuraMedia *Discusses common problems of the seriously ill and provides ideas that others have incorporated to promote a sense of well-being.*

Kauffman, Danette G. 1987. **Surviving Cancer : A Practical Guide for Those Fighting to Win**. Washington, D.C.: Acropolis Books Ltd. *A quick reference book of resources for the cancer patient, family, and friends plus lots of practical information and advice.*

Kushner, Harold S. 1981. **When Bad Things Happen to Good People**. New York: Schocken. *A rabbi out of his own suffering from death of handicapped child describes ways to view things in life. He decides God does not intend terrible things but is there with us.*

Lancaster, Matthew. 1985. **Hang Tough**. Garden City, NY: Paulist Press. *Written by a young cancer patient for other young cancer patients; describes the course of his illness.*

Sanford, Doris. 1986. **It Must Hurt A Lot**. Portland, OR: Multnomah Press. *The story of a little boy whose dog has died. Helps children relate to their own loss.*

Siegel, Bernie S. 1986. **Love, Medicine & Miracles**. New York: Harper & Row Publishers, Inc.

Viorst, Judith. 1971. **The Tenth Good Thing About Barney**. New York: Atheneum. *Describes the death of a cat to help children share their loss.*

❖ *Articles*

Fiore, Neil. "Bill of Rights for Family Members of Cancer Survivors" *An Almanac of Practical Resources for Cancer Survivors* (Mount Vernon, New York: Consumers Union, 1990) p. 148.

Holmes, J.H. and Rahe, R.H. 1967 "The Social Readjustment Rating Scale," *Journal of Psychosomatic Research*.

MacCannon, Doris and Diane Joyce "You've Got a Friend" Dec. 1990 *Health Progress*, page 60.

❖ *Other*

An Almanac Of Practical Resources for Cancer Survivors. 1990. Published by The National Coalition for Cancer Survivorship, Mt. Vernon, NY. *Practical information and insight and resources from health professionals and cancer survivors.*

A free single copy of **Chemotherapy and You : A Guide to Self-Help During Treatment** is available from the Office of Cancer Communications, National Cancer Institute, Building 31, Room 10A24, Bethesda, MD 20892. *This book helps the lay person understand chemotherapy and its side effects.*

For additional resources or assistance, contact the **US Department. of Health and Human Resources** or call **The Cancer Information Service** at 1-800-4-CANCER.

A free single copy of **Taking Time : Support for people with cancer and the people who care about them** is available from the Office of Cancer Communications, National Cancer Institute; Building

31; Room 10A24, Bethesda, Md. 20892. *An overview of life with cancer. Chapters on sharing cancer diagnosis, emotions, feelings, coping, getting the help you need. Offers suggestions and practical advice on how to keep life full.*

Information regarding the **State Library for the Blind and Physically Handicapped** can be had by calling 1-800-424-8567. They will give you information about services for persons who cannot read, hold, or turn the pages of a regular print book either short or long-term. Services are free, including mailings, cassette and record players, books, records, and tapes. They can tell you about special services, including recording textbooks for students with special needs and providing referrals for other services.

A free copy of the **Consumers Resource Handbook**, published by the United States Office of Consumer Affairs, is available by writing: Handbook, Consumer Information Center, Pueblo, Colorado, 81009. *Contains a wealth of information on health agencies, aging, insurance regulators, federal information centers and federal agencies.*

Other sources of information about cancer are: The Cancer Information Service (call 1-800-4-CANCER) the local library or hospital library.

ABOUT THE AUTHORS

Judy Griffith Ransom is a freelance writer and photographer whose work has appeared in numerous newspapers and magazines around the country. She lives with her family in Hendersonville, Tennessee. This is her first published book.

James G. Henderson is a principal in a business consulting and training firm based in Hendersonville, Tennessee, where he is very active in church and community affairs. He and his sons still live in Hendersonville. This is his first published book.